THE
NUT BUTTER
COOKBOOK

HarperCollins*Publishers*
1 London Bridge Street
London SE1 9GF

www.harpercollins.co.uk

First published by HarperCollins*Publishers* 2018

10 9 8 7 6 5 4 3 2 1

© HarperCollins*Publishers* 2018

Photographer: Joff Lee
Food Stylist: Mari Williams
Prop Stylist: Rebecca Newport

Heather Thomas asserts the moral right to be identified as the author of this work

A catalogue record of this book is available from the British Library

HB ISBN 978-0-00-831413-2
EB ISBN 978-0-00-831414-9

Printed and bound in Latvia

MIX
Paper from
responsible sources
FSC C007454

FSC™ is a non-profit international organisation established to promote the
responsible management of the world's forests. Products carrying the FSC
label are independently certified to assure consumers that they come from
forests that are managed to meet the social, economic and ecological needs
of present and future generations, and other controlled sources.

Find out more about HarperCollins and the environment at
www.harpercollins.co.uk/green

THE
NUT BUTTER
COOKBOOK

HEATHER THOMAS

HarperCollins*Publishers*

CONTENTS

INTRODUCTION

More and more of us are going nuts about nut butters as we embrace a healthier lifestyle and more wholesome diet. For many of us they have become a staple, and their popularity has expanded way beyond the familiar peanut butter we've all been eating for years. The choices now available are extremely diverse, and their natural, healthy image, nutritional benefits and range of flavours make them very appealing. Delicious, nutritious and energizing, these nut butters help to make us feel good about ourselves as well as doing us good – and tasting great!

WHY IS NUT BUTTER SO POPULAR?

The nut-butter market is a huge success story and it continues to grow rapidly at a global level. There are many reasons for this spectacular growth trend:

- Nut butters appeal to people who want a more natural, healthy and ethical plant-based diet, especially flexitarians, vegetarians and vegans.

- They are also popular with athletes and fitness-conscious foodies as they are nutrient-dense and a great source of protein for muscle building, maintenance and recovery. Plus, they are a more affordable way to boost nutrient and calorie intake compared with pricey protein bars and shakes.

- Because they have a very low GI (glycaemic index) rating, they help to provide slow-release, long-lasting energy for active lifestyles.

- Nut butters are also a useful tool in weight loss as eating even small amounts can leave us feeling full and prevent hunger pangs. Moreover, most brands these days are unsweetened and do not contain any added sugar.

GOOD FOR YOUR HEALTH

Nuts are among the world's healthiest foods and studies have shown that eating them regularly reduces the risk of developing heart disease, stroke and other age-related diseases. High in protein and heart-healthy omega-3 and -6 fats, nut butters are rich in vitamins as well as a range of essential minerals. They are also a good source of antioxidants, especially vitamin E, high in dietary fibre and low in sugar and carbs. Moreover, their poly-unsaturated and mono-unsaturated fat content helps to lower cholesterol and fight inflammation in the body.

Nut butters can help to lower blood pressure, protect against some cancers and build stronger bones and muscles. They also help to build and maintain a healthy immune system and support the structure and function of cells.

TYPES OF NUT BUTTERS

ALMOND BUTTER

Probably the healthiest of all the nut butters as it has fewer calories and more vitamin E and dietary fibre. Eaten for breakfast, it can stabilize blood-sugar levels for the rest of the day, making food cravings and snacking between meals less likely.

BRAZIL NUT BUTTER

Most of the fat content of Brazil nuts is mono-unsaturated, which is thought to lower LDL (bad cholesterol) and raise HDL (good cholesterol) in the bloodstream. It's also one of the highest natural sources of selenium, which is believed to fight inflammation and increase blood flow.

CASHEW BUTTER

Rich, smooth and creamy, this is one of the most popular alternatives to peanut butter, and although it's lower in protein, it's richer in minerals (calcium, magnesium and zinc) and other nutrients.

COCONUT BUTTER

This is richer and sweeter than other nut butters and quite oily. Although it can be used as a spread, it is more frequently added to smoothies, porridge and desserts.

HAZELNUT BUTTER

Most of us are familiar with the chocolatey variety of hazelnut spreads, but it's also available without flavourings. It's a good source of fibre, vitamin E, minerals and omega-6 fatty acids but only has half the protein of peanut butter. Turn to page 15 to try making your own!

MACADAMIA NUT BUTTER

This is low in saturated fat and contains a variety of healthy vitamins and minerals. It can help to lower unhealthy LDL cholesterol and control blood-sugar levels. Due to its high fibre content, it is gut friendly and may also ease the symptoms of irritable bowel syndrome (IBS).

PEANUT BUTTER

This is the most widely consumed nut butter in the world. It's highly nutritious, especially in protein, vitamin E and minerals, and available salted or unsalted, plain or with added flavourings, smooth or crunchy. Avoid brands that have added sugar and palm oil for the most nutritional benefits.

PECAN BUTTER

Although slightly higher in fat than other nut butters, this contains both omega-3 and -6 healthy fats, a jackpot of vitamins, minerals and dietary fibre.

PISTACHIO BUTTER

This is very nutritious and can help to keep our arteries healthy and reduce cholesterol in the body. It is an especially good source of potassium – just 25g (1oz) of pistachio butter can contain as much potassium as a banana.

WALNUT BUTTER

Walnuts are a great source of healthy omega-3 fats, which help stimulate leptin, the hormone that tells us when we've had enough to eat. This nut butter also has anti-inflammatory properties, making it a popular choice for people with autoimmune and inflammatory health problems.

COMBO BUTTERS

These can be made from grinding any of the nuts listed above and combining them with other nuts, edible seeds (sesame, pumpkin, sunflower, etc.) or flavourings, such as salt, honey, vanilla, spices and cocoa.

COOKING WITH NUT BUTTERS

Cooking with nut butters is not a new phenomenon – in Southeast Asia they've long known the benefits of cooking with nuts, especially peanuts. They are a staple of Malaysian and Thai food where they are sprinkled over noodles, curries and salads as well as playing the starring role in satay sauce. Nut butters can add flavour and texture as well as nutrients to both savoury and sweet dishes. Use them to make pasta sauces, dips, creamy soups, curries, salad dressings and drizzles.

And it's easy to make your own nut butters at home – just grind the nuts of your choice into a thick, oily paste. You can add flavourings, such as edible seeds, salt, honey and spices, if wished. We have basic recipes and suggestions to instruct and inspire you – all you need is a food processor.

BASIC RECIPES

BASIC RECIPES

It's so easy to make your own nut butters and, this way, you can get the quality, flavour and texture you really like while avoiding palm oil, sugar, salt and some of the other additives that are found in most shop-bought commercial brands.

For the best results and to give you more control over the taste, use shelled raw nuts and roast them in the oven yourself. They can be difficult to source but most wholefood, health-food and natural-food stores sell them.

Roasting the nuts not only enhances their flavour and aroma but it also releases their natural oils, making them easier to grind and giving a smoother texture.

To grind the nuts for any nut butter, you'll need a large, sturdy food processor. It takes a while for the nuts to release their oil and become smooth and creamy – as long as 10–15 minutes – so be patient. Be careful not to over-blitz the nuts or the nut butter will be too liquid and not spreadable. If you like crunchy peanut butter, you can remove a few spoonfuls in the early gritty stages of grinding and stir them in at the end.

HOMEMADE PEANUT BUTTER

Nothing compares with the natural goodness of homemade peanut butter, whether it's smooth and creamy or crunchy and nutty. This recipe shows you how you can adapt it to make either version, and it's a lot easier than you think.

MAKES 500G (1LB 2OZ)
PREP 10–15 MINUTES
COOK 10–15 MINUTES

500g (1lb 2oz/3½ cups) shelled raw peanuts
1 tbsp sunflower, vegetable or peanut (groundnut) oil
1–2 tbsp clear honey or agave syrup (optional)
sea salt (optional)

Preheat the oven to 180°C (160°C fan)/350°F/gas 4.

Put the nuts on a large baking tray (cookie sheet), spreading them out in a single layer, and roast for about 10–15 minutes until golden brown and fragrant. Remove from the oven and set aside to cool.

When the nuts are completely cold, blitz them in a food processor until they are coarse and gritty. At this stage you can remove some if you prefer a crunchy rather than a smooth, creamy texture.

Add the oil through the feed tube and keep blitzing, stopping occasionally to scrape down the sides of the processor bowl, until the nuts release their oils and you have a moist, creamy textured paste. Stir in the coarsely ground nuts, if you removed them earlier, together with salt and honey or agave, to taste (if using).

Store in a sterilized 500g (1lb 2oz) glass jar with a screw-top lid or a Mason jar and keep in the fridge for 1–2 months.

ALMOND, CASHEW AND MACADAMIA BUTTERS

To make cashew butter and almond butter or more unusual butters, such as hazelnut, walnut, macadamia nut, pecan or Brazil nut, follow the basic recipe above for peanut butter, adding salt and honey to taste. Roast and grind the nuts in exactly the same way until you have a creamy paste. If wished, you can use a combination of different nuts.

NUT AND SEED COMBO BUTTERS

For a more nutritious and crunchy paste, try blitzing the nuts with edible seeds, such as unsalted raw sunflower, sesame, chia, flax or pumpkin seeds.

Tip: To sterilize the jar, wash it in warm, soapy water, then rinse thoroughly. Put the jar and lid on a baking tray (cookie sheet) and leave in a low oven at 120°C (100°C fan)/the lowest gas mark for at least 30 minutes until completely dry. If you're using a Mason or Kilner jar, remove the rubber seal and wash separately in boiling water.

HAZELNUT AND COCOA SPREAD

This deliciously smooth chocolate and nut spread is a healthier and more wholesome version of the commercial spreads you can buy, many of which have added palm oil and lots of sugar. When you've tasted this, you'll never want to eat anything else. It's great spread on breakfast pancakes, crêpes and waffles as well as toast. And it's gluten-free and dairy-free, making it vegan-friendly.

MAKES 400G (14OZ)
PREP 10–15 MINUTES
COOK 10–15 MINUTES

400g (14oz/scant 3 cups) raw hazelnuts
1 tbsp sunflower, vegetable or peanut (groundnut) oil
2 tbsp good-quality unsweetened cocoa powder
a few drops of vanilla extract
2 tbsp clear honey, maple syrup or agave syrup
sea salt

Preheat the oven to 180°C (160°C fan)/350°F/gas 4.

Put the nuts on a large baking tray (cookie sheet), spreading them out in a single layer, and roast for about 10–15 minutes until golden brown and the skins are loose. Remove from the oven and set aside to cool.

Remove the skins by wrapping them in a sheet of kitchen paper (paper towel) and rubbing and rolling them around in it. Don't worry if some of the skins are a bit stubborn – just get most of them off and discard them.

Blitz the nuts in a food processor for about 10 minutes, stopping occasionally to scrape down the sides of the bowl, until the nuts release their oils and you have a moist, creamy, smooth paste.

Add the oil through the feed tube and keep blitzing, then add the salt, to taste, cocoa powder and vanilla. Blend again and then add the honey, maple syrup or agave. If it's not sweet enough for your taste, add a little more.

Store in a sterilized 400g (14oz) glass jar with a screw-top lid or a Mason jar and keep at room temperature for 3–4 weeks.

FLAVOURINGS

You can add a wide range of flavourings to the nut butters you make, depending on whether you like them salty, sweet, spicy, hot or aromatic. Experiment with some of the following...

- Sea salt or Himalayan salt
- Honey, maple syrup and agave syrup
- Fresh root ginger
- Spices: cardamom, cayenne, cinnamon, cloves, nutmeg, paprika (sweet or smoked), za'atar
- Vanilla: seeds or extract
- Dried crushed chilli flakes, chilli powder, hot sauces, e.g. Sriracha or Tabasco
- Citrus zest, e.g. lime or orange
- Dried and freeze-dried fruit, e.g. sour cherries and mango
- Cocoa, chocolate, espresso powder or coffee beans

BREAKFASTS AND BRUNCHES

FROZEN CASHEW BUTTER AND BANANA SMOOTHIE

You can whisk up a smoothie in less than 5 minutes, making it the perfect breakfast for people on the go. Smoothies are so versatile – you can add your favourite fruit, vegetables, flavourings and nut butters, of course (see the variations at the end of the recipe).

SERVES 1
PREP 5 MINUTES

2 tbsp cashew butter

1 tsp ground flaxseed (flaxseed meal)

1 frozen banana (see note)

120ml (4fl oz/½ cup) almond milk or vanilla soy milk

100g (4 oz/scant ½ cup) vanilla yoghurt

1 tsp clear honey (optional)

a few chia seeds, for sprinkling

Put all the ingredients except the chia seeds in a blender and blitz until thick and smooth.

Pour into a tall glass, sprinkle with chia seeds and drink immediately.

Note: Adding a frozen banana to a smoothie makes it thicker and more creamy. Before freezing bananas, always peel them and cut into chunks. Freeze overnight in a plastic bag. This makes it easier to add them to smoothies and you don't need a heavy-duty blender.

VARIATIONS

- Use peanut or almond butter instead of cashew butter.
- If you're a vegan and don't eat honey, use maple or agave syrup instead and a dairy-free vanilla yoghurt.
- Try adding some leafy spinach or kale, chopped dates, fresh berries, cocoa, hemp powder or ground cinnamon.

PEANUT BUTTER, DATE AND CINNAMON PROTEIN SHAKE

This health shake is high in protein and it's the perfect pick-me-up after a workout, as well as a nutritious breakfast. You can use any of your favourite nut butters (hazelnut works really well) and even add a banana (fresh or frozen) if you want to make it thicker.

SERVES 1
PREP 5 MINUTES

2 tbsp peanut butter
2 tbsp vanilla protein powder
2 tbsp rolled oats
2 medjool dates, stoned (pitted) and chopped
1 tbsp hemp seeds
¼ tsp ground cinnamon, plus extra for sprinkling
240ml (8½fl oz/1 cup) cold almond, soy or coconut milk
100g (4oz/scant ½ cup) 0% fat Greek yoghurt
ice cubes, to serve (optional)

Put all the ingredients in a blender and blitz until thick and smooth.

Pour into a tall glass, dust lightly with cinnamon and drink immediately, with or without ice.

VARIATIONS

- Instead of vanilla protein powder, try another flavour such as chocolate, or some rice protein powder.
- Vary the seeds: try flax, chia or pumpkin seeds.
- For a beautiful green result, add 1 teaspoon matcha powder.
- Instead of cinnamon, use milder ground cardamom.

ALMOND BUTTER PORRIDGE WITH BLUEBERRY COMPÔTE

Porridge is always a healthy and warming way to start the day and because it's high in fibre and low GI, it makes you feel full, so you're less likely to feel hungry and snack mid morning. The almond butter here gives it a delicious nutty, creamy flavour.

SERVES 4
PREP 5 MINUTES
COOK 10 MINUTES

85g (3oz/1 cup) rolled
   porridge oats
300ml (11fl oz/1¼ cups) water
240ml (8½fl oz/1 cup)
   unsweetened almond milk
a pinch of sea salt
3 tbsp almond butter
1–2 tsp honey or agave
   or maple syrup
thick yoghurt or nut cream,
   to serve

BLUEBERRY COMPÔTE
170g (6oz) frozen blueberries
1 tbsp water
1 tsp honey or agave or maple
   syrup

Make the blueberry compôte: put all the ingredients in a medium pan and set over a low heat. Stir gently from time to time until the blueberries thaw. They should be tender, not mushy, and still hold their shape.

Put the porridge oats, water, almond milk and salt in a non-stick saucepan and set over a low heat. Stir gently with a wooden spoon until the porridge oats are softened, then turn up the heat and, stirring all the time, bring to the boil. Reduce the heat and cook gently for 2–3 minutes until all the liquid has been absorbed and the porridge is thick, smooth and creamy.

Remove from the heat and stir in the almond butter. It will dissolve into the porridge. Sweeten to taste with honey, agave or maple syrup.

Divide the porridge among four breakfast bowls and spoon the blueberry compôte over the top. Serve with yoghurt or nut cream.

VARIATIONS
· Use cashew or peanut butter instead of almond butter.
· Top with fresh fruit, e.g. sliced banana, peach, apple or berries, or some chopped nuts, cacao nibs, seeds or dried fruit.

PEANUT BUTTER GRANOLA WITH FRUIT AND YOGHURT

Granola is really simple to make and it's healthier and tastes much better than most shop-bought varieties. This recipe makes enough for several breakfast servings if you can resist eating it as a snack from the jar! You can enjoy it with dairy, soy or nut milk, or with a fruit compôte or fresh fruit and yoghurt. It also makes a great topping, sprinkled over ice cream and creamy desserts.

MAKES APPROX. 500G (1LB 2OZ) GRANOLA
PREP 5 MINUTES
COOK 20–25 MINUTES

5 tbsp smooth peanut butter
2 tbsp coconut oil
4 tbsp honey or maple syrup
1 tsp ground cinnamon
340g (12oz/3½ cups) rolled oats
150g (5oz/scant 1 cup) coarsely chopped hazelnuts
50g (2oz/scant ½ cup) seeds, e.g. pumpkin or sunflower
fresh fruit, e.g. peaches, strawberries, raspberries, blueberries, to serve
0% fat Greek yoghurt or dairy-free coconut yoghurt, to serve

FLAVOURINGS (OPTIONAL)
chocolate chips
coconut shavings
raisins, dried cherries and cranberries
chopped dates, dried apricots and figs

Preheat the oven to 170°C (150°C fan)/325°F/gas 3. Line a baking tray (cookie sheet) with baking parchment.

Put the peanut butter, coconut oil, honey or maple syrup and cinnamon in a small pan set over a low heat. Stir gently for about 1–2 minutes until they melt and you have a smooth mixture.

Pour into a bowl and stir in the oats, hazelnuts and seeds until everything is well combined. If it seems a bit dry, just add some more honey or syrup. Spread out the mixture on the lined baking tray.

Bake in the oven for about 20–25 minutes or so, turning halfway, until golden brown. Don't worry if the granola isn't very crisp – it will get more crunchy as it cools. Remove from the oven and set aside.

When the granola is cool, store in an airtight jar or container. At this stage you can mix in some flavourings, if wished (as per the list). The granola will stay fresh for 3–4 weeks. Serve in bowls with fresh fruit and yoghurt.

VARIATION
· You can use almond or cashew butter instead of peanut and vary the nuts.

PEANUT BUTTER BREAKFAST PANCAKES

Breakfast pancakes are much easier to make than you think and much healthier than using a commercial pancake mix. You can prepare the batter in advance and let it stand until you're ready to cook. This recipe makes 8–12 pancakes depending on the size of your ladle.

SERVES 4
PREP 10 MINUTES
STAND 10 MINUTES
COOK ABOUT 15–20 MINUTES

2 large free-range eggs
330ml (11fl oz/generous 1¼ cups) dairy or unsweetened almond milk
1 tbsp maple syrup, plus extra for drizzling
175g (6oz/¾ cup) smooth peanut butter
225g (8oz/generous 2 cups) plain (all-purpose) flour
1 tbsp baking powder
¼ tsp ground cinnamon
a pinch of sea salt
vegetable oil, for spraying

TOPPINGS

sliced banana, fresh berries, dark (semi-sweet) chocolate chips, jam (jelly) or yoghurt, to serve

Beat the eggs, milk, maple syrup and peanut butter in a bowl until well combined and smooth.

Sift the flour, baking powder, cinnamon and salt into a mixing bowl. Make a hollow in the centre and pour in the peanut butter mixture. Beat until you have a smooth batter. Alternatively, use a food mixer to do this. Set aside to stand for at least 10 minutes.

Lightly spray a non-stick frying pan with some oil and set the pan over a medium heat. When it's hot, add a ladle of the peanut butter batter (two or even three ladles if it's a large pan) and cook for 1–2 minutes until bubbles appear on the surface and the pancake is set and golden underneath. Flip the pancake over and cook the other side. Wrap loosely in foil or keep warm in a low oven while you cook the remaining pancakes in the same way.

Serve the pancakes warm drizzled with maple syrup with the toppings of your choice.

PEANUT BUTTER BREAKFAST TOASTIES

A slice of toasted wholegrain or seedy bread spread with smooth or crunchy peanut butter and different toppings makes a quick and nutritious breakfast when you're in a hurry. Here are some ideas to inspire you and get you going!

PEANUT BUTTER AND HOT SAUCE TOASTIE

SERVES 1

PREP 5 MINUTES

1 medium slice wholegrain, multi-seed or wholewheat bread

1 heaped tbsp peanut butter

1 spring onion (scallion), finely chopped

a few sprigs of coriander (cilantro), chopped

a squeeze of lemon or lime juice

hot sauce, e.g. Sriracha or sweet chilli sauce, for drizzling

Toast the bread and spread with the peanut butter.

Sprinkle the spring onion and coriander over the top. Add a squeeze of lemon or lime juice and drizzle with hot sauce.

PEANUT BUTTER AND BANANA MAPLE TOASTIE

SERVES 1
PREP 5 MINUTES

1 small banana
1 heaped tbsp peanut butter
a pinch of ground cinnamon
1 medium slice wholegrain, multi-
    seed or wholewheat bread
maple syrup, for drizzling
nuts, chia seeds or cacao nibs,
    for sprinkling

Coarsely mash the banana with a fork and mix with the peanut butter and cinnamon.

Toast the bread and spread it with the banana peanut butter mixture.

Drizzle with maple syrup and sprinkle with the topping of your choice.

PEANUT BUTTER AND AVOCADO SMASH TOASTIE

SERVES 1
PREP 5 MINUTES

1 medium slice wholegrain, multi-
    seed or wholewheat bread
1 heaped tbsp peanut butter
1 small avocado, peeled, stoned
    (pitted) and coarsely mashed
honey, for drizzling (optional)

Toast the bread and spread with the peanut butter.

Top with the smashed avocado, spreading it out to the corners of the toast, and drizzle with honey, if using.

FRENCH TOAST WITH PEANUT BUTTER DRIZZLE

French toast is a delicious way of using up bread that's past its best. The peanut butter drizzle adds a touch of nutty sweetness to the savoury dipped and fried eggy bread. You can use vegetable oil instead of butter, if wished.

SERVES 4
PREP 10 MINUTES
COOK 5–6 MINUTES

2 large free-range eggs
120ml (4fl oz/½ cup) dairy or
  unsweetened soy or nut milk
a few drops of vanilla extract
½ tsp ground cinnamon
a pinch of ground nutmeg
a pinch of sea salt
4 thick slices wholegrain or
  multi-seed bread
unsalted butter, for frying
freshly ground black pepper
2 small bananas, sliced, to serve

PEANUT BUTTER DRIZZLE

3 tbsp maple syrup
75g (3oz/generous ¼ cup)
  crunchy peanut butter

Beat together the eggs, milk, vanilla, ground spices and salt in a bowl. Pour the mixture into a large shallow dish.

Dip the slices of bread (both sides) into the egg mixture and leave just long enough for the batter to penetrate the bread (usually less than 1 minute or 30 seconds each side). Don't leave it too long or it will get soggy and fall apart.

Heat the butter in a large frying pan (skillet) set over a medium heat. Add the soaked bread to the hot pan (do this in batches if necessary) and cook for 2–3 minutes until golden brown and crisp underneath. Turn the slices over and cook the other side.

Make the peanut butter drizzle: put the maple syrup and peanut butter in a small pan and stir gently over a low heat until melted and well combined.

Transfer the French toast to serving plates and top with a grinding of black pepper and the sliced bananas. Sprinkle with the peanut butter drizzle and serve hot.

VARIATIONS
• Use fresh berries, e.g. strawberries, raspberries, blueberries, instead of bananas.
• Serve with a spoonful of creamy soft cheese mixed with grated orange zest.

SEEDY CHOC CHIP ALMOND BUTTER GRANOLA BARS

These granola bars are a great breakfast when you're in a hurry and don't even have time for a bowl of cereal before leaving home. Alternatively, you can enjoy them as a healthy, energy-boosting snack at any time of the day. The bars will be less sweet and more crunchy if you use cacao nibs instead of chocolate.

MAKES 8 BARS OR 9 SQUARES
PREP 15 MINUTES
COOK 3–4 MINUTES
CHILL 1 HOUR

225g (8oz/1 cup) stoned (pitted) fresh dates
100g (4oz/generous 1 cup) roasted almonds (unsalted), coarsely chopped
125g (4½oz/scant 1½ cups) rolled oats
2 tbsp ground flaxseed (flaxseed meal)
2 tbsp chia seeds
50g (2oz/generous ¼ cup) dark (semi-sweet) chocolate chips or cacao nibs
60g (2oz/¼ cup) almond butter
5 tbsp honey or maple syrup
a few drops of almond or vanilla extract

Line a 20cm (8 inch) square cake tin (baking pan) with baking parchment.

Blitz the dates briefly in a food processor until you have a sticky purée. Transfer them to a mixing bowl and stir in the almonds, oats, seeds and chocolate chips.

Put the almond butter and honey in a small pan and set over a low heat. Warm through gently, stirring occasionally until the nut butter softens and the mixture blends.

Add the almond or vanilla extract and stir into the dry ingredients until well mixed and everything is evenly distributed.

Spoon the mixture into the lined tin, pressing it down evenly to level the top. Cover with kitchen foil or cling film (plastic wrap) and chill in the fridge for at least 1 hour until the mixture is firm.

Cut the mixture into bars or squares, remove from the tin and keep in an airtight container in the fridge or a cool place for up to 10 days.

VARIATIONS
· Add some dried cherries, cranberries, raisins or coconut flakes.
· Use peanut butter and chopped roasted peanuts instead of almonds.

FALAFEL WRAPS WITH PEANUT BUTTER PESTO

If you don't have time to make the falafels yourself, you can heat up some ready-made ones.
Almond or cashew butter makes a slightly more subtle version of the pesto.

SERVES 4
PREP 20 MINUTES
COOK 5–10 MINUTES

1 tsp cumin seeds
1 tsp coriander seeds
400g (14oz) can (1½ cups)
   chickpeas, rinsed and drained
1 carrot, grated
1 small red chilli, deseeded
   and diced
1 garlic clove, crushed
grated zest of 1 lemon
1 small bunch of flat-leaf parsley,
   finely chopped
2 tsp plain (all-purpose) flour
½ tsp baking powder
sea salt and black pepper
sunflower oil, for shallow frying
4 wholewheat tortilla wraps
crisp lettuce, tomatoes and
   cucumber, to serve
4 tbsp 0% fat Greek yoghurt, to
   serve (optional)

PEANUT BUTTER PESTO
1 large bunch of fresh basil (about
   2 cups)
120ml (4fl oz/½ cup) olive oil
2 garlic cloves, crushed
4 tbsp crunchy peanut butter
40g (1½oz/generous ¼ cup)
   grated Parmesan cheese
a squeeze of lemon juice

Make the peanut butter pesto: blitz all the ingredients in a blender until you have a thick green paste. Set aside while you make the falafels.

Toast the seeds in a small pan set over a medium heat for 1 minute until they release their fragrance. Remove immediately and blitz in a food processor with the chickpeas, carrot, chilli, garlic, lemon zest, parsley, flour, baking powder and some salt and pepper.

When you have a smooth, well-combined mixture, check the seasoning and then divide into 12 portions, shaping each one into a small ball.

Heat a little oil in a large frying pan (skillet) set over a medium heat. Cook the falafels, in batches, for about 2–4 minutes, turning occasionally, until golden brown all over. Remove and drain on kitchen paper (paper towels).

Warm the wraps on a griddle pan or in a low oven and divide the salad vegetables and falafels among them. Top with the yoghurt (if using) and drizzle with the peanut butter pesto. Roll up or fold over and serve warm.

SNACKS

PEANUT BUTTER PROTEIN BALLS

You can buy protein powder in most health-food stores. Ground flaxseed is not only gluten-free; it's also a great source of fibre and healthy omega-3 fatty acids.

MAKES APPROX. 24 BALLS
PREP 15 MINUTES
CHILL 1–2 HOURS

150g (5oz/⅔cup) smooth
    peanut butter
75g (3oz/¾ cup) rolled oats
50g (2oz/generous ¼ cup)
    diced dates
2 tbsp protein powder
5 tbsp ground flaxseed (flaxseed
    meal)
2 tbsp chia seeds
5 tbsp clear honey or maple syrup

Warm and soften the peanut butter in a microwave to make it easier to mix.

Stir in the other ingredients until you have a smooth, well-mixed dough. If the mixture is too sticky, add some more oats; if it's too dry, add some more honey, syrup or peanut butter.

Take small spoonfuls of the mixture and, with your hands, roll into small balls.

Place them on a large baking tray (cookie sheet) lined with baking parchment and chill in the fridge for 1–2 hours until set and then transfer to an airtight container. They will keep well in the fridge for 10–14 days.

CASHEW BUTTER ENERGY BALLS

Bite-sized energy balls make nutritious snacks. Any nut butter works well, use whatever you have handy.

MAKES APPROX. 30 BALLS
PREP 15 MINUTES
CHILL 1–2 HOURS

180g (6½oz/¾ cup) cashew butter
90ml (3fl oz/⅓ cup) clear honey
180g (6½oz/1¾ cups) rolled oats
30g (1oz/¼ cup) flaxseeds or chia
    seeds
60g (2oz/generous ¼ cup) dark
    (semi-sweet) chocolate chips
rolled oats or seeds, for coating

Put the cashew butter in a saucepan with the honey and stir gently over a low heat until it's just warm (not too hot) and well blended. Alternatively, you can do this in a microwave.

Remove from the heat and stir in the oats, seeds and chocolate chips, distributing them evenly. If the mixture is too sticky, add some more oats; if it's too dry, add some cashew butter.

Take small spoonfuls of the mixture and roll into small balls. Put some rolled oats or seeds in a shallow dish and roll the balls in them until they are sparsely coated all over.

Place them on a large baking tray (cookie sheet) lined with baking parchment, chill in the fridge for 1–2 hours until set and then transfer to an airtight container. They will keep well in the fridge for 10–14 days.

CHOCOLATE AND ALMOND BUTTER DATES

These make a great snack when you're feeling tired or your blood-sugar levels need a boost. You can use any nut or seed butter or a combo of both.

MAKES 12 DATES
PREP 10 MINUTES
COOK 5 MINUTES
FREEZE 15–20 MINUTES

12 medjool dates
60g (2oz/¼ cup) almond butter
150g (5oz/1 cup) dark (semi-sweet) chocolate (70% cocoa solids) broken into pieces

Cut down the side of each date and remove the stone (pit). Gently prise the date open and place a teaspoon of almond butter inside.

Melt the chocolate in a double boiler or heatproof bowl suspended over a pan of simmering water. Stir and remove from the heat.

Dip each date into the melted chocolate until half of it is covered. Remove and place on a baking tray (cookie sheet) lined with baking parchment.

Pop into the freezer for at least 15–20 minutes until the chocolate sets. Keep in the fridge in an airtight container.

VEGAN OPTION

CASHEW BUTTER AND BANANA TOASTIES

This is very nutritious and can be made in minutes. You can even eat it on the go!

SERVES 4
PREP 5 MINUTES

4 medium slices wholegrain or multi-seed bread
4 tbsp cashew butter
2 small bananas, sliced
2 tbsp chopped cashews or pistachios
ground cinnamon, for dusting
clear honey or maple syrup, for drizzling (optional)

Lightly toast the bread and spread with the cashew butter.

Top with the sliced banana and chopped nuts.

Dust with cinnamon and then drizzle with honey or maple syrup.

VARIATIONS
- Spread the toast with almond butter and top with sliced banana, toasted almonds and crunchy granola.
- Spread the toast with peanut butter and top with blueberries, then sprinkle with chia seeds.

CREAMY CASHEW BUTTER HUMMUS WITH ROASTED BEETS

Make this delicious tahini-free hummus with cashew butter. It will keep, covered, in the fridge for 2–3 days. If you're in a hurry and there's no time to roast the beetroot, serve it with raw vegetable dippers (peppers, celery, carrot sticks, fennel, cauliflower and broccoli florets).

SERVES 6
PREP 15 MINUTES
COOK 30–40 MINUTES

85g (3oz/scant ½ cup) cashew butter

2 x 400g (14oz) cans (3 cups) chickpeas, rinsed and drained

2 garlic cloves, crushed

1 tsp ground cumin

grated zest and juice of 1 lemon, plus extra juice for drizzling

2 tbsp olive oil, plus extra for drizzling

a pinch of smoked paprika, for dusting

1–2 tbsp mixed seeds, e.g. sesame, sunflower, pumpkin

sea salt

toasted pitta breads, cut into fingers, to serve

ROASTED BEETS

450g (1lb) raw beetroot (beets), peeled and cut into wedges

2 tbsp olive oil

1 tsp black mustard seeds

balsamic vinegar, for drizzling (optional)

sea salt

Preheat the oven to 220°C (200°C fan)/425°F/gas 7.

Toss the beetroot wedges with the oil and mustard seeds in a large bowl. Place them in a roasting pan and sprinkle with a pinch of sea salt. Cook in the preheated oven for 30–40 minutes until tender.

Make the hummus: put the cashew butter, chickpeas, garlic, cumin, lemon zest and juice and olive oil in a food processor. Blitz to a coarse-textured, grainy purée. If it is too thick, thin it with a little water, lemon juice or more olive oil. Season to taste with sea salt.

Spoon the hummus into a bowl and dust with paprika. Drizzle with olive oil and lemon juice and sprinkle the seeds over the top.

Serve the hummus with the roasted beets and fingers of toasted pitta bread.

VARIATIONS
- Use peanut or almond butter instead of cashew.
- For a creamier dip (for non-vegans), stir a little Greek yoghurt into the hummus before serving.

MANGO AND AVOCADO SPRING ROLLS WITH ALMOND BUTTER DIP

Eat these spring rolls as a snack or cut them diagonally into smaller portions and serve with pre-dinner drinks. You can get ahead and prepare everything in advance and assemble them later in the day. We've used almond butter but other nut butters work equally well.

SERVES 4–6
PREP 15 MINUTES

1 large ripe mango, peeled, stoned (pitted) and cut into strips

1 red (bell) pepper, deseeded and cut into strips

2 large carrots, cut into matchsticks

4 spring onions (scallions), shredded

85g (3oz/scant 1 cup) bean sprouts

1 large avocado, peeled, stoned (pitted) and diced

juice of 1 lime

1 tbsp soy sauce

a handful of mint or coriander (cilantro), chopped

12 rice paper wraps

dried chilli flakes, for sprinkling

ALMOND BUTTER DIP

100g (4oz/scant ½ cup) almond butter

1 tbsp soy sauce

juice of ½ lime

1 tbsp soft brown sugar or maple syrup

5 tbsp water

Make the almond butter dip: whisk all the ingredients together in a bowl, adding more water if needed, until the mixture is smooth and the consistency you want.

Mix together the mango, red pepper, carrots, spring onions, bean sprouts and avocado in a bowl. Toss lightly in the lime juice and soy sauce and fold in the mint or coriander.

Dip a rice wrapper into a bowl of warm water and soak briefly until it's pliable. Lay it out flat on a clean work surface and add some of the mango and avocado mixture. Fold the sides of the wrapper over the filling and roll up tightly like a parcel. Repeat with the rest of the wrappers and filling.

Serve the spring rolls with the almond butter dip, sprinkled with chilli flakes.

VARIATIONS

- Try adding cooked vermicelli rice noodles to make the spring rolls more substantial.
- Mix in some cooked prawns (shrimp) or shredded chicken.
- Vary the vegetables: try shredded greens, red cabbage or cucumber matchsticks.

SPICY PEANUT BUTTER BEANS ON TOAST

These homemade beans on toast are healthier and more delicious than the canned sort. They're so easy to make and if you're serving them for breakfastyou can top them with a poached egg for a non-vegan option.

SERVES 4
PREP 5 MINUTES
COOK 20 MINUTES

1 tbsp olive oil or peanut
   (groundnut) oil
1 large red onion, chopped
3 garlic cloves, crushed
2 tsp curry powder
400g (14oz/scant 2 cups) canned
   chopped tomatoes
400g (14oz/2 cups) canned
   cannellini or kidney beans,
   rinsed and drained
4 tbsp smooth peanut butter
4 medium slices wholegrain
   or multi-seed bread
chopped coriander (cilantro)
   or parsley, to garnish
sea salt and freshly ground black
   pepper

Heat the oil in a pan set over a low to medium heat and cook the onion and garlic for 6–8 minutes, stirring occasionally, until tender and golden.

Stir in the curry powder and cook for 1 minute. Add the tomatoes and beans and cook gently for about 10 minutes until the mixture reduces and thickens. Stir in the peanut butter and season with salt and pepper to taste. Warm through gently.

Toast the bread and top with the bean mixture. Sprinkle with coriander or parsley and eat immediately.

Tip: The amount of curry powder you use will depend on how mild or hot it is and your personal preference. You can substitute for curry paste or just add some diced fresh chilli or a pinch of dried chilli flakes or chilli powder instead.

CHICKEN, MANGO AND PEANUT BUTTER WRAPS

Wraps make a great snack or packed lunch. You can prepare the peanut butter drizzle in advance and assemble the wraps later. Use leftover roast chicken or buy a pack of ready-cooked breasts from the supermarket. If you want to serve this for supper, you can cook some chicken fresh on the griddle pan or barbecue and eat it warm with the salad and mango.

SERVES 4

PREP 15 MINUTES

COOK 2–5 MINUTES

4 cooked skinless chicken breast
   fillets, shredded or cut into
   chunks

1 large ripe mango, peeled, stoned
   (pitted) and diced

6 spring onions (scallions),
   chopped

a few sprigs of coriander
   (cilantro) or basil, chopped

4 wholewheat wraps or large
   tortillas

a large handful of crisp lettuce
   leaves, shredded

sea salt and freshly ground black
   pepper

PEANUT BUTTER DRIZZLE

100ml (4fl oz/⅓ cup) coconut
   cream

5 tbsp peanut butter

1 tbsp mango chutney

1 tbsp soy sauce

2 tsp grated fresh root ginger

a pinch of dried crushed chilli
   flakes

Make the peanut butter drizzle: mix all the ingredients together in a bowl, stirring until they are well blended and smooth.

In a bowl, mix together the chicken, mango, spring onions and coriander. Season lightly with salt and pepper.

Warm the wraps or tortillas in foil in a low oven or in a hot griddle pan for 1–2 minutes.

Scatter the lettuce over the wraps and top with the chicken and mango mixture. Drizzle lavishly with the peanut butter drizzle and roll up or fold over to enclose the filling.

VARIATIONS

· You can vary the fruit: use papaya (pawpaw) or pineapple instead of mango.
· Try crisp iceberg lettuce, wild rocket (arugula) or baby spinach leaves.
· Use cooked turkey, ham or pork instead of chicken.
· If you're a vegetarian or vegan, you could substitute griddled tofu or just mix some canned beans, red (bell) pepper, raw carrot and cucumber with the mango and spring onions.
· Almond butter works well, too.

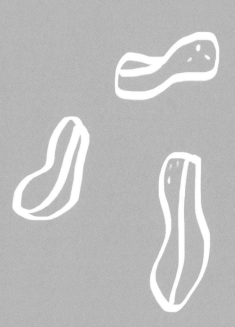

LIGHT MEALS
AND PACKED LUNCHES

FENNEL AND ORANGE SALAD WITH MISO CASHEW BUTTER DRESSING

This zingy, colourful salad will brighten up a winter day. You can cook the fennel and radicchio in an oiled griddle pan before mixing with the other ingredients and serve the salad warm.

SERVES 4
PREP 15 MINUTES

1 small fennel bulb, thinly sliced
1 radicchio, cored and thinly
   sliced or leaves torn
75g (3oz) tender kale, chopped
   or shredded
2 juicy blood oranges (ruby
   red oranges), peeled and
   segmented
30g (1oz/½ cup) roasted cashews
sea salt and freshly ground black
   pepper
1 tbsp black sesame seeds,
   to serve

MISO CASHEW BUTTER
   DRESSING
2 tbsp cashew butter
1 tbsp white miso paste
1 garlic clove, crushed
1 tbsp rice vinegar
1 tbsp mirin
2 tbsp olive oil
juice of 1 orange
1 tsp agave syrup

Make the miso cashew butter dressing: put all the ingredients in a blender and blitz until smooth and creamy. If it's too thick, thin it down with a little water.

Put the fennel, radicchio, kale, orange segments and cashews in a bowl. Toss lightly in the dressing and season to taste with salt and pepper.

Divide the salad among four plates and sprinkle with black sesame seeds.

VARIATIONS
• Add a handful of sprouted seeds to the salad.
• If blood oranges are out of season, use regular oranges instead or even ruby red grapefruit.
• Serve with some creamy goat's cheese.

WINTER COLESLAW WITH THAI PEANUT BUTTER DRESSING

You can eat this coleslaw as a light meal or it makes a good accompaniment
to griddled chicken, king prawns (jumbo shrimp) or tofu.

SERVES 4
PREP 10 MINUTES

2 carrots, cut into thin
  matchsticks or strips
1 Chinese cabbage (Napa
  cabbage), shredded
¼ red cabbage, shredded
½ cucumber, cut into thin strips
1 avocado, peeled, stoned
  (pitted) and cubed
a handful of coriander (cilantro),
  chopped

**THAI PEANUT BUTTER
DRESSING**

65g (2½oz/¼ cup) smooth peanut
  butter
2 tbsp peanut (groundnut) or
  vegetable oil
juice of 1 lime
1 tbsp nam pla (Thai fish sauce)
1 tbsp rice vinegar
1 tsp grated fresh root ginger
1 garlic clove, crushed
a pinch of dried crushed chilli
  flakes
1 tbsp soft brown sugar

Make the Thai peanut butter dressing: put all the ingredients
in a blender or food processor and blitz until smooth.

Put the carrots, Chinese cabbage, red cabbage, cucumber
and avocado in a bowl and mix gently together.

Pour the dressing over the coleslaw mixture and toss gently.
Sprinkle with coriander and serve.

VARIATIONS
- Use green or white cabbage, kale, chopped spring greens
  or thinly sliced broccoli.
- Add some chopped roasted peanuts to the salad.
- Stir in some grated onion, sliced spring onions (scallions)
  or thinly sliced red or yellow (bell) peppers.

BUCKWHEAT SALAD WITH LEMONY PEANUT BUTTER DRESSING

With its earthy, nutty flavour and crunchy texture, buckwheat is a healthy and nutritious grain to add to salads. What's more, it's gluten-free and easy to cook.

SERVES 4
PREP 15 MINUTES
COOK 10 MINUTES

150ml (5fl oz/⅔ cup) water
100g (3½oz/scant ¾ cup) roasted buckwheat (kasha)
2 tbsp sunflower seeds
2 tbsp sesame seeds
400g (14oz) tenderstem broccoli, trimmed and each stalk cut in half
60g (2oz/scant 1 cup) sun-blush tomatoes in olive oil, drained and chopped
100g (4oz) mixed sprouted seeds, e.g. alfalfa, broccoli, radish
1 avocado, peeled, stoned (pitted) and thinly sliced
a pinch of dried chilli flakes
1 small bunch of chives, snipped
sea salt and freshly ground black pepper

LEMONY PEANUT BUTTER DRESSING
3 tbsp smooth peanut butter
½ tsp grated fresh root ginger
juice of 1 lemon
1 tbsp soy sauce
1 tbsp maple syrup

Make the lemony peanut butter dressing: beat all the ingredients together in a bowl or jug until well blended and creamy.

In a saucepan bring the water to the boil. Reduce the heat to a bare simmer and stir in the buckwheat. Cook gently, covered but stirring occasionally, for 6–8 minutes until the buckwheat is just tender but not mushy. Set aside, covered, for 2–3 minutes, then spread the cooked buckwheat out on a large plate or baking tray (cookie sheet) and leave to cool.

Toast the seeds in a small frying pan (skillet) set over a medium heat for 1–2 minutes, tossing gently, until golden brown and they release their aroma. Remove from the pan and set aside.

Steam the broccoli in a steamer or a colander over a pan of simmering water for 3–5 minutes until it is just tender but still retains some 'bite'.

Gently mix the warm broccoli with the buckwheat, sun-blush tomatoes, sprouted seeds and avocado in a large bowl. Toss gently in the dressing and season to taste with salt and pepper.

Divide the salad among four serving plates and sprinkle with the chilli flakes, chives and toasted seeds. Serve immediately.

VARIATIONS
- Instead of sun-blush tomatoes, use cherry or baby plum ones.
- Sprinkle the salad with some crumbled feta, ricotta or goat's cheese.
- Use orange or lime juice instead of lemon.

NOODLE, BROCCOLI AND TOFU PEANUT BUTTER JARS

The secret of successful jar salads is the order in which they are layered. Always put the dressing at the bottom and then add noodles or grains, followed by firmer vegetables and protein in the middle and leafy greens and salad leaves at the top, to prevent them getting soggy.

SERVES 4
PREP 15 MINUTES
COOK 5–10 MINUTES

250g (9oz) fine egg noodles (dried weight)

250g (9oz) broccoli, cut into small florets

225g (8oz) smoked tofu, cubed

olive oil, for spraying

175g (6oz) frozen soya beans, defrosted in boiling water

½ small Chinese cabbage (Napa cabbage), shredded

4 spring onions (scallions), chopped

sweet chilli sauce, for drizzling (optional)

PEANUT BUTTER DRESSING

4 tbsp peanut butter

1 garlic clove, crushed

2 tbsp light soy sauce or tamari

1 tbsp peanut (groundnut) oil

1 tbsp rice wine vinegar

a pinch of dried crushed chilli flakes

a splash of water, to mix

Make the peanut butter dressing: whisk all the ingredients together until smooth and creamy, adding more water if needed. Pour into the bottom of four small Mason or Kilner jars.

Cook the egg noodles as per the instructions on the pack. Drain and cool.

Steam the broccoli in a steamer basket or colander placed over a pan of simmering water for about 3 minutes until just tender and still bright green.

Pat the tofu dry with kitchen paper (paper towels). Lightly spray a small frying pan (skillet) with olive oil and place over a high heat. Add the tofu to the hot pan and cook for a few minutes, turning it occasionally, until golden brown all over. Remove from the pan and allow to cool.

Put the noodles on top of the dressing in the jars and then layer the soya beans, tofu and broccoli on top. Finish with the Chinese cabbage and spring onions.

When you're ready to eat the salad, either shake or stir the jar to toss everything in the peanut dressing, or tip the contents into a bowl and stir gently. Serve with a drizzle of chilli sauce, if wished.

KALE AND CHICKPEA SALAD IN PEANUT BUTTER DRESSING

Raw kale is highly nutritious and packed with nutrients but it can be quite bitter. Rubbing some oil and lemon juice into it will soften and moisten the leaves and make them less bitter. If you have a sweet tooth, just add some more honey or maple syrup to the dressing.

SERVES 4
PREP 15 MINUTES

300g (10oz) kale, torn or
   shredded
1 tbsp olive oil
1 tsp lemon juice
1 large ripe avocado, peeled,
   stoned (pitted) and diced
1 red apple, cored and diced
400g (14oz) can (1½ cups)
   chickpeas, rinsed and drained
150g (5oz) creamy goat's cheese,
   crumbled or diced
sea salt and freshly ground black
   pepper

**MUSTARDY PEANUT
   BUTTER DRESSING**
3 tbsp peanut butter
1 garlic clove, crushed
1 heaped tsp honey mustard
1 tsp clear honey or maple syrup
juice of 1 lemon
3 tbsp olive oil

Make the mustardy peanut butter dressing: blitz all the ingredients in a blender until smooth or shake in a screw-top jar until blended.

Put the kale in a large bowl and gently massage the oil and lemon juice into it with your fingers.

Add the avocado, apple and chickpeas and then toss gently in the dressing. Season to taste with sea salt and black pepper.

Divide among four serving plates and top with the goat's cheese.

VARIATIONS
· Use spinach, rocket or radicchio instead of kale.
· Add some chopped walnuts, pecans, peanuts or toasted
   pine nuts and seeds.
· Top with crumbled blue cheese, e.g. Roquefort or feta.

STIR-FRIED CHILLI BROCCOLI WITH QUICK SATAY SAUCE

If you can't get the slender tenderstem broccoli for this dish, don't despair. You can use purple sprouting or even regular calabrese instead. Just break it into bite-sized florets before cooking.

SERVES 4
PREP 10 MINUTES
COOK 15–20 MINUTES

1 tbsp peanut (groundnut) or
   sesame oil
750g (1lb 10oz) tenderstem
   broccoli, trimmed and halved
   lengthways if thick
2 garlic cloves, thinly sliced
2.5cm (1 inch) piece fresh root
   ginger, peeled and diced
1 red chilli, deseeded and diced
1 tbsp nam pla (Thai fish sauce)
cooked basmati rice, to serve

SATAY SAUCE

1 tsp peanut (groundnut) oil
2.5cm (1 inch) piece fresh root
   ginger, peeled and diced
1 red chilli, deseeded and diced
1 shallot, chopped
2 garlic cloves, crushed
1 tbsp muscovado (soft dark
   brown) sugar
4 tbsp crunchy peanut butter
200ml (7fl oz/generous ¾ cup)
   coconut milk
2 tbsp dark soy sauce
juice of 1 lime

Make the satay sauce: heat the oil in a saucepan set over a medium to high heat. Cook the ginger, chilli, shallot and garlic, stirring occasionally, for 2–3 minutes until softened.

Stir in the sugar, peanut butter, coconut milk and soy sauce and simmer gently, stirring occasionally, for about 10 minutes until the sauce reduces and thickens. Remove from the heat and stir in the lime juice. Cover the pan and set aside.

Heat the oil in a wok or deep frying pan (skillet) set over a medium to high heat. Add the broccoli and a splash of water and stir-fry briskly for 2–3 minutes until it's just starting to get tender. Add the garlic, ginger and chilli and stir-fry for 1 minute. Add the nam pla and continue stir-frying for 1 minute.

Serve the broccoli immediately in shallow bowls with some plain boiled rice. Spoon the satay sauce over the top.

VARIATIONS
- Stir-fry some thinly sliced red (bell) pepper, spring onions (scallions) and cashews or peanuts along with the broccoli.
- For a really hot and spicy satay sauce, add 1 tablespoon Thai red curry paste.

PEANUT BUTTER, RED PEPPER AND SPINACH QUESADILLAS

If you've never considered adding peanut butter to quesadillas, now's the time to try it.

SERVES 4
PREP 15 MINUTES
COOK 25–30 MINUTES

2 large red (bell) peppers
2 garlic cloves, crushed
4 spring onions (scallions),
   chopped
1 tbsp vegetable or olive oil,
   plus extra for brushing
a pinch of dried crushed chilli
   flakes
a large handful of spinach,
   chopped
2 tomatoes, diced
1 ripe avocado, peeled, stoned
   (pitted) and diced
4 large tortillas
2 tbsp crunchy peanut butter
50g (2oz/½ cup) grated Cheddar
   or Monterey Jack cheese
sea salt and freshly ground
   black pepper
guacamole and lime wedges,
   to serve

Place the red peppers under a preheated overhead grill (broiler), turning them occasionally, until the skin is blistered all over and starting to char. Pop them into a plastic bag and leave them to cool. Peel them, removing the seeds and cores, and cut the flesh into strips.

Cook the garlic and spring onions in the oil in a frying pan (skillet) for 2–3 minutes. Add the chilli flakes and spinach, then cover the pan with a lid and cook for 1 minute until the leaves wilt. Stir in the tomatoes and avocado and seasoning to taste.

Lightly brush a griddle pan with oil and set over a medium heat. Add one of the tortillas to the pan and spread with a spoonful of peanut butter. Add half the red peppers and half the spinach mixture, then sprinkle half the cheese over the top. Cover with another tortilla, pressing down well.

Cook for 3–4 minutes until golden underneath, then carefully turn the quesadilla over and cook the other side until golden brown and the cheese has melted. Remove from the pan and cook the other quesadilla in the same way.

Cut each quesadilla into six wedges and serve immediately with some guacamole and lime wedges for squeezing.

VARIATIONS
• Serve with soured cream and pico de gallo or drizzled with chilli sauce.
• Use a hot Mexican chilli instead of crushed flakes.

STIR-FRIED SHRIMP COURGETTI WITH PEANUT BUTTER SAUCE

Spiralized vegetables are a slimming alternative to pasta and noodles and surprisingly filling. Vegetarians can substitute extra vegetables or tofu for the tiger prawns.

SERVES 4
PREP 15 MINUTES
COOK 5 MINUTES

4 courgettes (zucchini)
2 carrots
1 tbsp peanut (groundnut)
   or vegetable oil
2 garlic cloves, crushed
1 red chilli, diced
450g (1lb) raw tiger prawns
   (shrimp)
a handful of coriander (cilantro),
   chopped
40g (1½oz/¼ cup) roasted
   peanuts
sea salt and freshly ground black
   pepper
cooked rice, to serve (optional)

PEANUT BUTTER SAUCE
4 tbsp smooth peanut butter
1 tbsp sesame oil
1 tbsp rice vinegar
1 tbsp soy sauce
1 tsp clear honey or maple syrup
juice of 1 lime

Make the peanut butter sauce: beat all the ingredients together in a bowl or jug until well blended and creamy.

Spiralize the courgettes and carrots using blade C. Alternatively use a julienne peeler or a mandolin slicer if you prefer thicker 'noodles'.

Heat the oil in a wok or deep frying pan (skillet) set over a medium heat. Add the courgettes and carrots and stir-fry for 2 minutes.

Stir in the garlic and chilli and add the prawns. Cook, tossing occasionally, for about 2 minutes until they turn pink. Stir in the peanut butter sauce, adding a little water if it's too thick, and cook for 1 minute – just long enough to heat through. Check the seasoning.

Stir in the coriander and divide among four serving bowls. Sprinkle with peanuts and serve with rice (if using).

SPICY SWEET POTATO WEDGES WITH CURRIED PEANUT BUTTER DIP

· ·

These sweet potato wedges make a great snack, pre-dinner nibble or party food. You can cook everything in advance and reheat them just before you're ready to serve.

SERVES 4
PREP 10 MINUTES
COOK 25–30 MINUTES

600g (1lb 5oz) sweet potatoes
2 tbsp olive oil
a pinch of cayenne, chilli powder
    or dried crushed chilli flakes
a pinch each of ground cumin
    and turmeric
a few sprigs of coriander
    (cilantro), chopped
sea salt and freshly ground
    black pepper

CURRIED PEANUT BUTTER DIP
2 tbsp peanut (groundnut) oil
4 spring onions (scallions),
    chopped
2 garlic cloves, crushed
1 red Thai chilli, diced
3 tbsp crunchy peanut butter
1 tbsp dark brown sugar
2 tsp Thai red curry paste
4–5 tbsp water, to mix

Preheat the oven to 200°C (180°C fan)/400°F/gas 6.

Wash and scrub the sweet potatoes – there's no need to peel them. Pat dry with kitchen paper (paper towels) and cut each one into thick wedges. Arrange on a large baking tray (cookie sheet) and drizzle with oil. Turn them in the oil until they are glistening all over.

Sprinkle with a good pinch of sea salt, black pepper and the ground spices. Bake in the preheated oven for 25–30 minutes until tender inside but crisp and golden brown on the outside.

Meanwhile, make the curried peanut butter dip: heat the oil in a pan set over a medium heat. Cook the spring onions, garlic and chilli, stirring, for 3–4 minutes until softened. Stir in the peanut butter and sugar and cook for 1 minute. Add the curry paste and water and keep stirring until you have a hot and well-blended dipping sauce. Remove from the heat and set aside to cool.

Serve the warm sweet potato wedges, sprinkled with coriander, with the dip on the side.

BALSAMIC ONIONS WITH CREAMY PEANUT SAUCE

Sticky caramelized onions and shallots can be eaten on their own as a light meal or served as an accompaniment to roast chicken or lamb. Alternatively, you can add other vegetables and even fruit to the baking dish – try aubergine (eggplant), peppers and fresh figs.

SERVES 4
PREP 10 MINUTES
COOK 35 MINUTES

2 red onions, peeled and cut into wedges
8 shallots, peeled
2 tbsp olive oil
3 tbsp balsamic vinegar
1 tbsp demerara sugar
4 griddled flatbreads or wraps
sea salt and freshly ground black pepper
rocket (arugula) or crisp salad leaves, to serve

CREAMY PEANUT SAUCE
225g (8oz/scant 1 cup) crunchy peanut butter
240g (8½oz/1 cup) 0% fat Greek yoghurt
1 tbsp hot sauce, e.g. Sriracha
1 tsp clear honey

Preheat the oven to 180°C (160°C fan)/350°F/gas 4.

Put the red onions and shallots in a baking dish and toss them in the olive oil. Drizzle with the balsamic vinegar and season with salt and pepper.

Cook in the preheated oven for about 30 minutes until tender, sticky and starting to colour. Sprinkle with the sugar and pop back in the oven for another 5 minutes.

Meanwhile, make the creamy peanut sauce: mix the peanut butter with the yoghurt and then stir in the hot sauce and honey.

Serve the onions and shallots with griddled flatbreads or rolled up in wraps with the creamy peanut sauce, with some salad leaves on the side.

BAKED CAULIFLOWER WITH CASHEW BUTTER

You can buy a packet or small jar of ready-made tandoori spice blend in most supermarkets and delis. Alternatively you can make your own with ground spices – you just need a mixture of cumin, ginger, coriander, paprika, cayenne and turmeric plus garlic powder. Adding a fresh chilli to the cashew butter mixture will give it some real heat.

SERVES 4
PREP 10 MINUTES
COOK 40 MINUTES

125g (4½oz/½ cup) cashew butter
2 tbsp coconut oil
1 tbsp tandoori spice blend
a pinch of ground turmeric
1 red chilli, deseeded and diced
    (optional)
juice of 1 lime
1 large cauliflower, trimmed and
    separated into florets
a handful of coriander (cilantro),
    chopped
sea salt
cooked rice and griddled chicken
    or salmon (optional), to serve

Preheat the oven to 180°C (160°C fan)/350°F/gas 4. Line a baking tray (cookie sheet) with foil or baking parchment.

In a bowl, mix together the cashew butter, coconut oil, tandoori spice blend, turmeric, chilli (if using) and enough lime juice to make a smooth paste.

Add the cauliflower and turn it in the spicy mixture until the florets are coated all over. If it's too thick, you can thin it down with some water or more lime juice.

Arrange the cauliflower florets on the lined baking tray and bake in the preheated oven for about 40 minutes until cooked, tender and golden brown.

Serve hot, sprinkled with sea salt and coriander, with rice and griddled chicken or salmon, if you like.

VARIATIONS
· Use peanut or almond butter instead.
· Serve sprinkled with chopped roasted cashews.
· Use peanut (groundnut) oil instead of coconut oil.

BANG BANG CHICKEN

Crisp, crunchy and refreshing, this classic Chinese salad is a great way of using up leftover cooked chicken (or turkey). You can substitute cashew or almond butter in the dressing and scatter the finished dish with roasted cashews or pistachios.

SERVES 4
PREP 20 MINUTES
COOK 5–10 MINUTES

200g (7oz) rice noodles
   (dried weight)
150g (5oz) bean sprouts
1 large carrot, cut into strips
   with a vegetable peeler
4 spring onions (scallions), shredded
1 ripe mango, peeled, stoned
   (pitted) and cubed
100g (4oz) pak choi (bok choy),
   thinly sliced
400g (14oz) cooked chicken
   breasts, skinned and shredded
a handful of coriander (cilantro),
   chopped
50g (2oz/scant ½ cup) coarsely
   chopped roasted peanuts
1 red chilli, deseeded and
   shredded

PEANUT BUTTER DRESSING
65g (2½oz/¼ cup) crunchy
   peanut butter
60ml (2fl oz/¼ cup) boiling water
1 tbsp each toasted sesame oil, soy
   sauce, Sriracha or sweet chilli
   sauce and rice wine vinegar
2 tsp maple syrup
1 tsp grated fresh root ginger
juice of 1 lime

Cook the noodles according to the instructions on the packet. Drain well.

Put the bean sprouts, carrot, spring onions, mango, pak choi, chicken and coriander in a large bowl and mix together.

Make the peanut butter dressing: stir the peanut butter and boiling water in a pan set over a low heat until melted and blended. Pour into a bowl and beat in the remaining ingredients. If it's too thick, thin it down with a little more water.

Mix the rice noodles into the chicken and vegetables. Drizzle the peanut butter dressing over the top and toss gently.

Divide the salad among four serving plates and sprinkle with the peanuts and chilli. Serve immediately.

DINNERS

ROASTED PUMPKIN AND NUTTY QUINOA

You can eat this hot for supper or cold the following day (it makes a great packed lunch, too). Experiment with different roasted vegetables including butternut squash, aubergine (eggplant), carrots, beetroot (beets) and vine tomatoes.

SERVES 4
PREP 20 MINUTES
COOK 20–25 MINUTES

450g (1lb) pumpkin, peeled, deseeded and cubed
1 large red onion, cut into wedges
olive oil, for drizzling
leaves stripped from a few thyme sprigs
½ tsp sweet paprika
350g (12oz/2 cups) quinoa (dry weight)
juice of 1 lemon
150g (5oz/1 cup) roasted cashews
a handful of coriander (cilantro) or parsley, chopped
60g (2oz) feta cheese, crumbled
sea salt and freshly ground black pepper

CASHEW DRIZZLE
60g (2oz/¼ cup) cashew butter
60g (2oz/¼ cup) tahini
1 tsp sweet paprika
a pinch of cayenne pepper
6 tbsp water

Preheat the oven to 200°C (180°C fan)/400°F/gas 6.

Put the pumpkin and red onion in a roasting pan or baking dish and drizzle with olive oil. Sprinkle with the thyme leaves and dust with paprika. Toss gently to coat everything in the oil.

Roast in the preheated oven for 20–25 minutes until the vegetables are tender.

Meanwhile, cook the quinoa according to the instructions on the packet.

Make the cashew drizzle: beat the cashew butter, tahini and spices in a bowl until well combined. Whisk in the water until you have a smooth mixture. You can add more water if it's too thick for drizzling. Add salt to taste.

Put the roasted vegetables in a serving bowl and gently mix in the quinoa, lemon juice, cashews and chopped herbs. Season to taste with salt and pepper.

Serve warm, topped with the crumbled feta and sprinkled with the cashew drizzle.

THAI GREEN VEGETABLE CURRY WITH PEANUT BUTTER

Ground peanuts are often used to thicken and flavour curries, sauces and stews in Asian cuisine. The addition of peanut butter makes this spicy vegetable and coconut curry even more creamy.

SERVES 4
PREP 10 MINUTES
COOK 20–25 MINUTES

2 tbsp peanut (groundnut) or
    vegetable oil
1 red onion, thinly sliced
200g (7oz) small Thai aubergines
    (eggplants), quartered
    lengthways
3 garlic cloves, crushed
2.5cm (1 inch) piece fresh root
    ginger, peeled and diced
1 lemongrass stalk, peeled and
    finely sliced
1–2 tbsp Thai green curry paste
    (according to taste)
300g (10oz) baby plum or cherry
    tomatoes, halved
240ml (8½fl oz/1 cup) canned
    coconut milk
4 fresh lime leaves, thinly sliced
2 tsp nam pla (Thai fish sauce)
1 tbsp brown sugar
3 tbsp smooth peanut butter
250g (9oz) fine green beans,
    trimmed and halved
150g (5oz) baby spinach leaves
a handful of coriander (cilantro)
    or Thai basil, chopped
2 tbsp chopped roasted peanuts
cooked white rice, to serve

Heat the oil in a large deep frying pan (skillet) set over a medium heat and cook the onion and aubergines, stirring occasionally, for 6–8 minutes until softened and golden.

Add the garlic, ginger and lemongrass and cook for 1 minute. Stir in the curry paste, add the tomatoes and cook for 2–3 minutes. Add the coconut milk, lime leaves, nam pla, brown sugar and peanut butter. Simmer for at least 5 minutes until the liquid reduces slightly. If the curry seems too thick, add some more coconut milk or vegetable stock to thin it.

Stir in the green beans and spinach. Cook for 2–3 minutes – just long enough for the green beans to become tender and the spinach to wilt into the curry and turn bright green. Stir in the chopped herbs.

Serve the curry sprinkled with chopped roasted peanuts on a bed of steamed or boiled rice

VARIATIONS
- You can add some chicken or prawns (shrimp).
- Use red curry paste instead of green.
- Add a dash of lime juice or serve with quartered fresh limes.

CHICKPEA ALMOND VEGGIE BURGERS

These veggie burgers can be made in advance and kept chilled in the fridge overnight, or frozen in batches. We've used almond butter but any nut butter works well. You can add a few chopped nuts, too, for a more crunchy texture.

SERVES 4
PREP 15 MINUTES
COOK 16–20 MINUTES

3 tbsp olive oil
1 red onion, finely chopped
2 garlic cloves, crushed
2 x 400g (14oz) cans (3 cups)
   chickpeas, rinsed and drained
3 tbsp almond butter
150g (5oz) kale, shredded
a handful of coriander (cilantro)
   or parsley, chopped
grated zest of 1 lemon
1 medium free-range egg, beaten
3 tbsp mayonnaise, plus extra
   to serve
a few drops of hot sauce, e.g.
   Sriracha
4 seeded burger buns
shredded lettuce and sliced
   tomato
sea salt and freshly ground
   black pepper

Heat 2 tablespoons oil in a frying pan (skillet) set over a low to medium heat and cook the onion and garlic for 8–10 minutes until softened but not coloured.

Transfer to a blender or food processor and add the chickpeas, almond butter, kale, herbs, lemon zest, salt and pepper and some of the beaten egg. Blitz to a coarsely textured mixture that you can shape into burgers. If it's too dry, add some more egg or a little lemon juice to moisten it. Divide into four portions and, with your hands, shape each one into a burger.

Heat the remaining oil in a large non-stick frying pan set over a medium heat. When it's hot, add the burgers and cook for about 4–5 minutes each side until lightly browned and heated right through.

Meanwhile, mix the mayonnaise with hot sauce to taste.

Split the burger buns in half and fill each one with a burger, some lettuce and sliced tomato and a spoonful of mayonnaise.

VARIATIONS
- Use spinach instead of kale.
- Serve with sweet chilli sauce or mango chutney instead of mayonnaise.

TOFU PAD THAI WITH CASHEW BUTTER SAUCE

We've used tofu to make a zingy vegetarian pad thai, but it works equally well with cooked chicken or prawns (shrimp). Traditionally, roasted peanuts are used but cashews make a delicious alternative. You could even use a mixed nuts and seeds combo butter.

SERVE 4
PREP 10 MINUTES
COOK 10 MINUTES

250g (9oz) flat rice noodles
    (dry weight)
2 tbsp peanut (groundnut) oil
3 garlic cloves, crushed
2.5cm (1 inch) piece fresh root
    ginger, peeled and diced
8 spring onions (scallions), sliced
1 red bird's eye chilli, diced
250g (9oz) firm tofu, cubed
100g (4oz/1 cup) bean sprouts
3 tbsp crushed roasted cashews
2 tbsp sesame seeds
a handful of coriander (cilantro)
    or Thai basil, chopped
lime wedges and sweet chilli
    sauce, to serve

CASHEW BUTTER SAUCE
5 tbsp cashew butter
2 tbsp soy sauce
1 tbsp nam pla (Thai fish sauce)
2 tbsp brown sugar or agave syrup
1 tbsp tamarind paste
grated zest and juice of 1 lime
2–3 tbsp water

Mix together all the ingredients for the cashew butter sauce in a bowl.

Prepare the rice noodles according to the instructions on the packet.

Heat the oil in a wok or deep frying pan (skillet) set over a medium to high heat. Add the garlic, ginger, spring onions and chilli and stir-fry briskly for 1 minute. Add the tofu and cook for 5 minutes, turning several times, until golden all over. Stir in the cashew butter sauce, then reduce the heat, cover the pan and cook for 2 minutes.

Add the rice noodles and bean sprouts and stir them gently into the sauce and tofu mixture. Stir-fry for 1 minute, tossing them lightly.

Divide the mixture among four shallow serving bowls. Sprinkle with the roasted nuts, sesame seeds and chopped coriander or Thai basil. Serve hot with lime wedges for squeezing and some sweet chilli sauce.

CHICKPEA AND VEG ABUNDANCE BOWL

Bowl food is so healthy and delicious and you can add almost anything you like. How about toasted nuts or seeds, a spoonful of tahini, hummus or yoghurt or a few drops of chilli sauce?

SERVES 4
PREP 15 MINUTES
COOK 30–35 MINUTES

2 x 400g (14oz) cans (3 cups) chickpeas, rinsed and drained
½ tsp ground cumin
½ tsp chilli powder
5 tbsp olive oil
1 large red onion, cut into wedges
2 red or yellow (bell) peppers, deseeded and cut into chunks
450g (1lb) sweet potatoes, peeled and cubed
200g (7oz) cherry tomatoes
3 whole garlic cloves, unpeeled
a few sprigs thyme and rosemary
200g (7oz) kale, trimmed and large stems removed
a handful of coriander (cilantro) or parsley, chopped
cooked brown rice, bulgur wheat or quinoa, to serve
1 ripe avocado, peeled, stoned (pitted) and thinly sliced
sea salt and black pepper

ALMOND BUTTER DRESSING
2 tbsp almond butter
2 tbsp balsamic vinegar
1 tbsp maple syrup
1 tsp honey mustard
juice of ½ lemon

Preheat the oven to 200°C (180°C fan)/400°F/gas 6.

Put the chickpeas in a bowl with the ground cumin, chilli powder and a pinch of sea salt. Toss lightly in 2 tablespoons olive oil. Spread them out in a single layer on a baking tray (cookie sheet) and roast in the preheated oven for about 20 minutes, turning once or twice, until golden brown and slightly crisp. Remove and cool a little.

Meanwhile, put the red onion, peppers, sweet potatoes and tomatoes in a large roasting pan. Tuck the garlic down between the vegetables and sprinkle with the thyme and rosemary. Drizzle with the remaining oil and season with salt and pepper.

Roast in the preheated oven for 25–30 minutes or until the vegetables are tender. Add the kale to the pan, stirring it into the roasted vegetables, and return to the oven for 5 minutes. Discard the herbs and squeeze the garlic cloves out of their skins into the vegetable mixture. Stir in the chopped coriander or parsley.

While the vegetables are cooking, make the almond butter dressing: whisk the ingredients together until smooth, or shake vigorously in a screw-top jar. If it's too thick, add a little water.

Divide the chickpeas and vegetables among four shallow serving bowls, together with some brown rice, bulgur wheat or quinoa. Top with the avocado and drizzle with almond butter dressing.

PASTA RIBBONS WITH PESTO

It's so easy to make your own pesto, and even if you don't have a food processor you can use a blender or traditional pestle and mortar. We are all familiar with the classic sauce made from pounded toasted pine nuts, but how about using nut butter instead for an intensely aromatic and creamier version?

SERVES 4
PREP 15 MINUTES
COOK 10 MINUTES

500g (1lb 2oz) tagliatelle or
    fettuccine (dry weight)
1 ripe avocado, peeled, stoned
    (pitted) and diced
50g (2oz/½ cup) walnuts or
    pecans, roughly chopped
    (not too small)
grated Parmesan cheese,
    for sprinkling

NUT BUTTER PESTO

200g (7oz/2 cups) basil leaves,
    stalks removed
2 garlic cloves, crushed
3 tbsp nut butter, e.g. walnut,
    pecan or almond
50g (2oz/½ cup) grated
    Parmesan cheese
grated zest and juice of 1 lemon
120ml (4fl oz/½ cup) fruity
    olive oil
sea salt and freshly ground
    black pepper

Make the nut butter pesto: put the basil leaves, garlic, nut butter, Parmesan, lemon zest and juice in a food processor and pulse briefly to chop the basil.

With the lid on and the motor running, add the olive oil gradually in a thin, steady stream through the feed tube until you have a bright green paste, which is neither too thick nor too thin. Season with salt and pepper to taste.

If you're not using the pesto straight away, pour it into a screw-top jar or a sealable plastic container and cover it with a thin layer of olive oil. This will keep the colour fresh. You can store it in the fridge for up to a week.

Cook the pasta according to the instructions on the packet. Drain well and return to the pan. Add the pesto and toss gently to coat all the strands. Gently stir in the avocado and nuts, distributing them throughout.

Serve the pasta in shallow serving bowls, sprinkled with Parmesan.

VARIATIONS
· Add some chopped sun-blush tomatoes to the pasta.
· Sprinkle with some dried crushed chilli flakes.
· Mash an avocado into the pesto sauce just before tossing with the pasta and serving.

TOFU AND PEANUT BUTTER CURRY

This healthy dish is not only gluten- and dairy-free, but vegan-friendly too. You can buy tofu (soya bean curd) in solid blocks and it's a great source of plant protein, vitamin B1 and a wide range of minerals.

SERVE 4
PREP 10 MINUTES
COOK 20–25 MINUTES

2 tbsp peanut (groundnut) oil
1 large onion, finely chopped
1 red (bell) pepper, deseeded
    and thinly sliced
2 garlic cloves, crushed
2.5cm (1 inch) piece fresh root
    ginger, peeled and diced
1 tbsp curry paste
1 tsp ground turmeric
240ml (8½fl oz/1 cup) coconut
    milk
120ml (4fl oz/½ cup) vegetable
    stock
60g (2oz/¼ cup) smooth peanut
    butter
400g (14oz) firm tofu, drained,
    rinsed and cubed
200g (7oz) fine green beans
    or broccoli florets
a handful of Thai basil or
    coriander (cilantro), chopped
2 tbsp chopped roasted peanuts
cooked rice and lime wedges,
    to serve

Heat the oil in a large saucepan set over a medium heat. Cook the onion, red pepper, garlic and ginger, stirring occasionally for about 5 minutes until the vegetables start to soften.

Stir in the curry paste and turmeric and cook for 1 minute. Add the coconut milk, stock and peanut butter and bring to the boil. Reduce the heat and simmer for 10 minutes.

Stir in the tofu and the beans or broccoli and continue cooking gently for 5–10 minutes until the beans are tender and the sauce has reduced and thickened. If it's too thick, thin it down to your liking with more stock or water. Gently stir in the Thai basil or coriander.

Serve the curry sprinkled with chopped peanuts on a bed of rice with lime wedges for squeezing.

VARIATIONS
· You can use almost any vegetables in this curry – try cauliflower florets, chunks of aubergine (eggplant), shredded kale or cherry tomatoes.
· Add more curry paste or a diced chilli for more heat or serve with a shake of Sriracha hot sauce or sweet chilli sauce.

CHICKEN SATAY WITH SPICY CASHEW BUTTER

Using cashew butter to make the sauce gives it a slightly milder and more subtle flavour than the usual peanuts. To make this dish you will need eight long, thin wooden skewers. Soak them in cold water before using to prevent them burning. You can even prepare the chicken a day ahead and leave it to marinate overnight.

SERVES 4
PREP 15 MINUTES
MARINATE 30 MINUTES
COOK 35 MINUTES

75ml (2½fl oz/generous ¼ cup) coconut milk
1 tsp ground cumin
1 tsp ground turmeric
1 tsp ground coriander
2 garlic cloves, crushed
2 tsp brown sugar
500g (1lb 2oz) skinless chicken breast fillets, cut into long 3cm (1 inch) wide strips
sea salt
cooked rice, to serve

CASHEW BUTTER SATAY SAUCE

100g (4oz/scant ½ cup) cashew butter
2 tsp Thai red curry paste
300ml (11fl oz/1¼ cups) canned coconut milk
2 tbsp brown sugar or palm sugar
juice of 1 lime

Mix together the coconut milk, ground spices, garlic, brown sugar and a pinch of sea salt in a bowl to make the marinade. Stir in the chicken strips, mix well and then cover and marinate in the fridge for at least 30 minutes – preferably longer.

Thread the chicken strips onto eight soaked wooden skewers, weaving them through the chicken to make 'S' shapes.

Make the cashew butter satay sauce: put the cashew butter, curry paste and coconut milk in a pan set over a low heat. Stir gently until you have a well blended mixture. Add the sugar and lime juice and simmer for about 15 minutes or so until the sauce has thickened (if it's too thick, just add a little water or more coconut milk). Transfer to a bowl and set aside to cool slightly.

Cook the chicken skewers on a hot griddle pan or a barbecue over a medium heat for about 15 minutes, turning occasionally, until golden brown, slightly charred and cooked right through. Serve hot with the satay sauce and some cooked rice.

VARIATION
• Use crunchy peanut butter to make the sauce.

GRIDDLED CHICKEN AND CASHEW BUTTER FAJITAS

Who would have thought that nut butter could taste so good in fajitas? For a vegetarian version just omit the chicken and add some griddled courgette (zucchini), carrot, sweet potato or asparagus.

SERVES 4
PREP 10 MINUTES
COOK 12–18 MINUTES

peanut (groundnut) or vegetable
   oil, for brushing
2 large red onions, thinly sliced
2 red or green (bell) peppers,
   deseeded and thinly sliced
450g (1lb) chicken breast fillets,
   cut into chunks
4 large flour or corn tortillas
4 heaped tbsp cashew butter
a few crisp Cos (romaine) lettuce
   leaves, shredded
a handful of coriander (cilantro),
   roughly chopped
4 tbsp grated Monterey Jack
   or Cheddar cheese
sour cream and guacamole,
   to serve

PICO DE GALLO
3 large ripe tomatoes, diced
1 red chilli, diced
½ red onion, diced
1 small bunch of coriander
   (cilantro), finely chopped
juice of 1 lime
sea salt

Make the pico de gallo: mix all the ingredients together in a bowl and set aside.

Lightly brush a large, non-stick, ridged griddle pan with oil and set over a medium heat. Add the red onions and peppers and cook for 6–8 minutes, turning occasionally, until tender, slightly charred and the onions are starting to caramelize. Remove from the pan and keep warm.

Add the chicken to the pan and cook for 8–10 minutes, stirring occasionally, until golden brown all over and cooked right through. Remove from the pan.

Heat the tortillas in the hot pan – just long enough to warm them through. Or you can warm them in the microwave or wrapped in foil in a low oven.

Spread the tortillas with the cashew butter. Add the lettuce, coriander, cooked chicken, peppers and onions. Sprinkle with grated cheese and add some pico de gallo. Roll up the tortillas and eat immediately with sour cream and guacamole.

STIR-FRIED CHICKEN WITH CASHEW BUTTER SAUCE

The cashew butter sauce is so easy to make and gives a delicious nutty and creamy finishing touch to this healthy stir-fry. Peanut butter and roasted peanuts work equally well.

SERVES 4
PREP 10 MINUTES
COOK 12 MINUTES

250g (9oz) egg noodles
(dry weight)
1 tbsp peanut (groundnut)
or vegetable oil
500g (1lb 2oz) chicken breast
fillets, cubed
1 red chilli, shredded
2 garlic cloves, crushed
1 tsp grated fresh root ginger
125g (4½oz) tenderstem
broccoli, trimmed and halved
lengthways
1 large carrot, cut into
matchsticks
2 heads pak choi (bok choy),
sliced
1 bunch of spring onions
(scallions), sliced
1 large courgette (zucchini),
sliced into ribbons with a
potato peeler
100g (4oz/generous ½ cup)
roasted cashews

CASHEW BUTTER SAUCE

100g (4oz/scant ½ cup) cashew
butter
2 tbsp soy sauce
90ml (3fl oz/⅓ cup) water

Make the cashew butter sauce: mix together all the ingredients in a bowl and set aside.

Cook the egg noodles according to the instructions on the packet. Drain well.

Meanwhile, heat the oil in a wok or deep frying pan (skillet) set over a medium to high heat. Add the chicken and stir-fry for 5 minutes until golden brown all over.

Add the chilli, garlic, ginger, broccoli and carrot and stir-fry briskly for 3–4 minutes until just tender but still crisp. Stir in the pak choi, spring onions and courgette and stir-fry for 2 minutes.

Gently stir in the cooked noodles, roasted cashews and cashew butter sauce. Divide among four serving bowls and serve immediately.

PEANUT BUTTER CHICKEN TRAY BAKE WITH CHILLI GREENS

One-pan meals are easy to prepare and cook and there's no washing up. You can vary the vegetables – try using small new potatoes, carrots, onion wedges and cherry tomatoes.

SERVES 4
PREP 15 MINUTES
COOK 35–40 MINUTES

4 tbsp smooth peanut butter
1 tsp grated fresh root ginger
2 tbsp soy sauce
1 tbsp rice vinegar
1 tsp peanut (groundnut) or
    vegetable oil, plus extra
    for drizzling
grated zest and juice of 1 lime
4 boneless chicken breasts
1 red (bell) pepper, deseeded and
    cut into chunks
1 yellow (bell) pepper, deseeded
    and cut into chunks
1 aubergine (eggplant), cut into
    chunks
400g (14oz) sweet potato,
    peeled and cut into wedges
a handful of Thai basil or
    coriander (cilantro), chopped
sea salt and freshly ground
    black pepper
cooked rice, to serve

CHILLI GREENS
400g (14oz) kale, green cabbage
    or spring greens, shredded
2 tsp peanut (groundnut) or
    vegetable oil
2 garlic cloves, crushed
1 red chilli, shredded

Preheat the oven to 200°C (180°C fan)/400°F/gas 6.

Mix together the peanut butter, ginger, soy sauce, vinegar, oil, lime zest and juice until you have a smooth paste. Slash each chicken breast two to three times with a knife and rub the paste into the cuts and all over.

Place the chicken, peppers, aubergine and sweet potato in a large ovenproof dish or roasting pan. Drizzle with oil and season with salt and pepper. Bake in the preheated oven for 35–40 minutes, turning the chicken and vegetables once or twice. When the chicken is cooked right through and the skin is crisp and golden brown and the vegetables are tender, remove from the oven.

Meanwhile, make the chilli greens: cook the greens in a large pan of boiling water for 1 minute, then drain in a colander, rinse under running cold water and squeeze out any excess liquid. Pat dry with kitchen paper (paper towels).

Heat the oil in a wok or frying pan (skillet) set over a medium heat. Cook the garlic and chilli, without colouring, for 1 minute and then add the greens. Stir-fry for 2 minutes and season lightly with salt and pepper.

Serve the chicken and vegetables sprinkled with the chopped Thai basil or coriander with the chilli greens and rice.

MALAYSIAN PRAWN AND PEANUT BUTTER LAKSA

This is bowl food at its most spicy and best. You can scatter some chopped roasted peanuts over the top.

SERVE 4
PREP 15 MINUTES
COOK 10–15 MINUTES

200g (7oz) vermicelli rice
   noodles (dried weight)
1 tbsp peanut (groundnut) oil
400ml (14fl oz/scant 1¾ cups)
   canned coconut milk
500ml (17fl oz/2 cups) fish or
   vegetable stock
1–2 tbsp nam pla (Thai fish sauce)
juice of 1 lime
675g (1lb 8oz) raw peeled large
   prawns (jumbo shrimp)
250g (9oz) mangetout or sugar
   snap peas, halved lengthways
a handful of coriander (cilantro),
   chopped
4 spring onions (scallions), sliced
1 red chilli, deseeded and sliced

PEANUT BUTTER LAKSA PASTE
2 tbsp smooth peanut butter
2 red Thai chillies
2 stalks lemongrass, peeled
   and chopped
4 shallots, diced
3 garlic cloves
4 fresh kaffir lime leaves, shredded
5cm (2 inch) piece fresh root
   ginger, peeled and chopped
2 tsp ground turmeric
1 tsp palm sugar or brown sugar
a handful of coriander (cilantro)
   leaves and stalks

Make the peanut butter laksa paste: blitz everything in a food processor or blender until thick and smooth.

Soak the rice noodles according to the instructions on the packet. Drain well.

Heat the oil in a large saucepan set over a low to medium heat. Add the laksa paste and stir for 2 minutes or until it releases its aroma – take care not to let it brown or burn. Add the coconut milk and stock and bring to the boil. Reduce the heat to a simmer and stir in the nam pla, lime juice and prawns. Simmer gently for 4–5 minutes until the prawns turn pink.

Meanwhile, steam the mangetout or sugar snap peas, or cook them briefly in boiling water, until just tender but still al dente with a lovely fresh green colour. Drain and add to the laksa with the coriander.

Divide the noodles among four shallow serving bowls and ladle the laksa over the top. Sprinkle with the spring onions and chilli and serve.

CASHEW BUTTER PASTA WITH GARLIC SHRIMP AND GREENS

Pasta cooked in this way makes a delicious supper when you don't have much time to cook. Most of the ingredients come from the store cupboard or freezer so there's not much shopping. If you don't have cashew butter and cashews, substitute peanuts instead.

SERVES 4
PREP 5 MINUTES
COOK 8–10 MINUTES

500g (1lb 2oz) spaghetti or linguine (dried weight)
1 tbsp olive oil
1 bunch spring onions (scallions), chopped
4 garlic cloves, crushed
675g (1lb 8oz) raw peeled large prawns (jumbo shrimp), fresh or frozen and thawed
200g (7oz) baby leaf spinach
a handful of flat-leaf parsley or chives, chopped
4 tbsp chopped roasted cashews
freshly ground black pepper

CASHEW BUTTER SAUCE
75g (3oz/generous ¼ cup) cashew butter
90ml (3fl oz/⅓ cup) boiling water
3 tbsp light soy sauce
1 tbsp rice vinegar
1–2 tbsp sweet chilli sauce

Make the cashew butter sauce: mix all the ingredients together in a bowl until well blended and smooth.

Cook the pasta according to the instructions on the packet. Drain well.

Meanwhile, heat the oil in a large frying pan (skillet) set over a medium heat. Add the spring onions and garlic and cook for 2–3 minutes until softened but not coloured. Stir in the prawns and cook, turning them over occasionally, for 3–4 minutes until pink all over. Add the spinach and cook for 1–2 minutes until it wilts and turns bright green. Take the pan off the heat.

Add the cooked pasta and the cashew butter sauce to the pan and toss everything together gently. Sprinkle with the chopped parsley or chives and some black pepper.

Divide among four shallow serving bowls and serve immediately, sprinkled with cashews.

SALMON AND NUTTY GINGER RICE NOODLES

Salmon cooked this way makes a really quick and easy supper dish. For the best flavour and maximum nutritional benefit, use wild salmon fillets, rather than farmed ones, if you can find them.

SERVES 4
PREP 5 MINUTES
COOK 10–15 MINUTES

250g (9oz) rice noodles (dried weight)
1 tbsp peanut (groundnut) oil
4 salmon fillets, skinned
1 bunch of spring onions (scallions), finely chopped
1 red chilli, deseeded and thinly sliced
2 tbsp toasted sesame seeds
a handful of coriander (cilantro), chopped

NUTTY GINGER SAUCE
2 tbsp almond, peanut or cashew butter
2 tbsp dark soy sauce
1 tbsp grated fresh root ginger
1 tsp sesame oil
1 tsp clear honey
juice of 1 lime

Mix all the nutty ginger sauce ingredients together in a bowl until smooth and well blended.

Cook the rice noodles according to the instructions on the packet. Drain well.

Meanwhile, heat the oil in a large non-stick frying pan (skillet) or griddle pan and set over a medium heat. Add the salmon fillets and cook for about 10 minutes or so, turning halfway, until cooked through. Add the spring onions and chilli and cook for 1 minute until softened.

Toss the hot rice noodles with the nutty ginger sauce and then add the salmon, spring onions and chilli. Use a fork to gently break up the salmon into smaller pieces and distribute it among the noodles.

Divide the mixture among four shallow serving bowls and sprinkle with toasted sesame seeds and coriander before serving.

BAKING
AND DESSERTS

SALTED CHOC AND CASHEW BUTTER COOKIES

You can make the cookie dough in advance and chill it in the fridge until you're ready to bake the cookies, or you can even keep some in the freezer.

MAKES APPROX. 16 COOKIES
PREP 15 MINUTES
CHILL 2 HOURS
COOK 15 MINUTES

200g (7oz/scant 1 cup)
    cashew butter
200g (7oz/scant 1 cup) butter
    at room temperature
150g (5oz/¾ cup) demerara sugar
seeds from 1 split vanilla pod
2 medium free-range eggs
300g (10oz/3 cups) plain
    (all-purpose) flour
2 tsp baking powder
2 tbsp cocoa powder
1½ tsp crunchy sea salt flakes
200g (7oz/1¼ cups) dark (semi-
    sweet) chocolate chips

Beat the cashew butter, butter, sugar and vanilla seeds together until light, fluffy and creamy. It's best to use a hand-held electric whisk or a food mixer for this. Gradually beat in the eggs, a little at a time, and then add the flour, baking powder, cocoa and sea salt flakes. Keep beating until the mixture is well blended and smooth. Fold in the chocolate chips, distributing them throughout the mixture.

Use your hands to roll the dough into a ball and remove from the bowl. Wrap it up in a large piece of baking parchment, twisting the ends of the paper to enclose it, and chill in the fridge for at least 2 hours or, better still, overnight until firm.

Preheat the oven to 170°C (150°C fan)/325°F/gas 3. Line two baking trays (cookie sheets) with baking parchment.

Cut the dough into 16 equal portions and roll each one into a ball. Place them in rows on the lined baking trays, leaving a little space in between. Press down lightly on each ball to spread it out into a circle.

Bake in the preheated oven for about 15 minutes until cooked, golden brown and slightly firm to the touch. Cool on a wire rack and store in a tin, jar or other airtight container for up to 1 week.

WHITE CHOC CHIP MACADAMIA NUT BUTTER COOKIES

We've used mild macadamia nut butter and whole nuts to make these cookies.
To make your own nut butter, see page 14.

MAKES APPROX. 25 COOKIES
PREP 15 MINUTES
COOK 10–15 MINUTES

125g (4½oz/generous ½ cup)
    butter at room temperature
185g (6½oz/¾ cup) macadamia
    nut butter
200g (7oz/1 cup) soft
    brown sugar
2 medium free-range eggs,
    beaten
a few drops of vanilla extract
200g (7oz/2 cups) plain
    (all-purpose) flour
½ tsp baking powder
½ tsp bicarbonate of soda
    (baking soda)
175g (6oz/1 cup) white
    chocolate chips
50g (2oz/scant ½ cup)
    macadamia nuts
sea salt

Preheat the oven to 180°C (160°C fan)/350°F/gas 4. Line two baking trays (cookie sheets) with baking parchment.

Beat the butter, macadamia nut butter and sugar together until light, fluffy and creamy. It's best to use a hand-held electric whisk or a food mixer for this. Gradually beat in the eggs, a little at a time, and then add the vanilla, flour, baking powder, bicarbonate of soda and a pinch of salt. Keep beating until the mixture is well blended and smooth.

Fold in the white chocolate chips and the macadamia nuts. The mixture should be the consistency of a soft dough.

Take small portions of the dough – about the size of a heaped teaspoon – and roll each one into a ball. Place them in rows on the lined baking trays, leaving a little space in between. Press down lightly on each ball to spread it out into a circle.

Bake in the preheated oven for 10–15 minutes until cooked, golden brown and slightly firm to the touch. Cool on a wire rack and store in a tin, jar or other airtight container for up to 1 week.

VARIATION
· Alternative flavourings include grated orange zest, a pinch each of ground cinnamon and nutmeg or a little strong espresso coffee.

CHOCOLATE PEANUT BUTTER RICE CRISPIE BARS

As an alternative to coating these sweet treats with chocolate, you can stir some dark chocolate chips into the peanut butter mixture before chilling, or even add some chopped nuts and dried cranberries, blueberries, cherries or raisins. Maple or agave syrup can be substituted for honey.

MAKES 9 SQUARES
PREP 10 MINUTES
COOK 5 MINUTES

120ml (4fl oz/½ cup) clear honey
50g (2oz/¼ cup) butter
125g (4½oz/½ cup) smooth
    peanut butter (unsalted)
100g (4oz/4 cups) rice cereal,
    e.g. Rice Krispies
225g (8oz) dark (semi-sweet)
    chocolate, broken into pieces

Line a square 20cm (8 inch) cake tin (baking pan) with baking parchment.

Put the honey, butter and peanut butter in a large saucepan set over a low to medium heat. Stir gently until the two butters melt and blend with the honey.

Remove from the heat and stir in the rice cereal, turning it gently until it's completely coated.

Spoon the mixture into the lined cake tin, pressing down gently to spread it into the corners and level the top. Cover and leave in the fridge until chilled and set.

Melt the chocolate in the microwave or in a heatproof bowl suspended over a pan of simmering water. When it's melted and smooth, spread it evenly over the peanut butter mixture.

Leave to set, either at room temperature or in the fridge if you want to speed this up. Cut into squares before serving. Store them in an airtight container in the fridge or a cool place for 4–5 days.

VEGAN FUDGY NUT BUTTER BROWNIES

These squidgy, nutty brownies are made without the usual dairy products: eggs and butter. Instead we've used flaxseed 'eggs' and nut butter. If preferred you could use ground chia seeds to make the 'eggs'.

MAKES 9 SQUARES
PREP 15 MINUTES
STAND 5 MINUTES
COOK 25–30 MINUTES

150g (5oz/¾ cup) soft brown sugar
125g (4½oz/½ cup) almond, pecan or smooth peanut butter
175g (6oz/1 cup) dark (semi-sweet) chocolate chips
a few drops of vanilla extract
125g (4½oz/1¼ cups) self-raising flour
½ tsp bicarbonate of soda (baking soda)
½ tsp sea salt
125g (4½oz/1 cup) chopped walnuts or pecans

FLAX 'EGGS'
2 tbsp ground flaxseed (flaxseed meal)
5 tbsp water

Preheat the oven to 180°C (160°C fan)/350°F/gas 4.
Line a square 20cm (8 inch) cake tin (baking pan) with baking parchment.

Make the flax 'eggs': stir the ground flaxseed and water in a bowl and set aside for at least 5 minutes until it congeals and becomes gelatinous and thickened. Alternatively, pulse in a food processor.

Put the sugar, nut butter, chocolate chips and vanilla in a saucepan set over a low heat and stir gently until the nut butter and chocolate melt and the sugar dissolves.

Add to the flax 'eggs' mixture and beat well. Beat in the flour, bicarbonate of soda and sea salt. You should end up with a smooth batter. If it's too thick, thin it with a little water or almond milk. Stir in the chopped nuts.

Pour the batter into the prepared tin and bake in the preheated oven for about 25–30 minutes until it's set on top and the edges are shrinking away from the sides of the tin. Don't worry if it's still a bit wobbly and moist in the middle.

Leave to cool in the tin and when it's completely cold, cut into squares. Serve the brownies on their own or with vegan nut cream and fruit. Store in an airtight container for up to 4 days.

SEEDY PEANUT BUTTER SQUARES

These crunchy peanut butter squares are surprisingly filling and make a delicious snack – much healthier than a chocolate bar or potato chips. And they're quick and easy to make, too.

MAKES 9 SQUARES
PREP 10 MINUTES
COOK 30–35 MINUTES

125g (4½oz/½ cup) butter
125g (4½oz/½ cup) crunchy
  peanut butter
4 tbsp clear honey or agave syrup
2 ripe bananas, mashed
225g (8oz/2¼ cups) rolled
  porridge oats
100g (4oz/scant ¾ cup) dried
  apricots, chopped
25g (1oz/scant ¼ cup) dried
  cherries or cranberries
25g (1oz/scant ¼ cup) chia seeds
25g (1oz/scant ¼ cup) sesame
  seeds
a few drops of vanilla extract
a pinch of sea salt

Preheat the oven to 160°C (140°C fan)/325°F/gas 3. Lightly butter a 20cm (8 inch) square baking tin (pan) and line with baking parchment.

Gently stir the butter, peanut butter and honey or agave syrup in a pan set over a low heat until the butter melts.

Remove from the heat and stir in the bananas, oats, dried fruit, seeds and vanilla until you have a sticky mixture. If it's not firm enough, add some more oats; if it's not sticky enough, add more honey or agave syrup.

Transfer the mixture to the prepared tin, pressing it down well with the back of a metal spoon to level the top. Bake in the preheated oven for 25–30 minutes until crisp and golden brown.

Remove and leave to cool in the tin before cutting into squares. Store in an airtight container for up to 4 days.

VARIATIONS
· Vary the seeds: try pumpkin, sunflower, flax and poppy seeds.
· Use raisins, sultanas (golden raisins) or chopped dates.
· Add some chopped peanuts or chocolate chips to the mixture.

SKINNY PEANUT BUTTER FLAPJACKS

There's no fat in these high-fibre healthy flapjacks. The dates and their soaking liquid together with maple syrup or honey are used to bind the mixture. Use peanut butter with no-added sugar and jumbo oats for the best results.

MAKES 8 BARS OR 16 SQUARES
SOAK 10+ MINUTES
PREP 10 MINUTES
COOK 20–25 MINUTES

100g (4oz/½ cup) stoned (pitted) dates
¾ tsp bicarbonate of soda (baking soda)
150g (5oz/⅔ cup) smooth peanut butter
2 egg whites
120ml (4fl oz/½ cup) maple syrup or honey
400g (14oz/4 cups) rolled porridge oats
1 tsp ground cinnamon
50g (2oz/generous ¼ cup) raisins
25g (1oz/scant ¼ cup) sunflower seeds
25g (1oz/scant ¼ cup) pumpkin seeds

Preheat the oven to 180°C (160°C fan)/350°F/gas 4. Line a 30 x 20cm (12 x 8 inch) cake tin (baking pan) with baking parchment.

Put the dates and bicarbonate of soda in a heatproof dish and cover with boiling water. Leave to soften and then drain the dates, reserving the soaking liquid.

Blitz the peanut butter, dates, egg whites and maple syrup or honey in a food processor until you have a smooth mixture.

In a mixing bowl, combine the peanut butter mixture with the porridge oats, cinnamon, raisins and seeds. The mixture should be sticky. If it's too dry, mix in some of the reserved soaking liquid.

Spoon the mixture into the prepared tin and press it down evenly and into the corners. Bake in the preheated oven for about 20–25 minutes until crisp and golden brown.

Remove from the oven and allow to cool in the tin before cutting into 8 bars or 16 squares. Remove and store in an airtight container for up to 5 days.

PEANUT BUTTER CHOCOLATE CHIP MUFFINS

Everyone will love these moist, nutty muffins studded with gooey chocolate. For a double chocolate version, just add 2 tablespoons cocoa powder to the mix.

MAKES 12 MUFFINS
PREP 15 MINUTES
COOK 25–30 MINUTES

100g (4oz/scant ½ cup) smooth peanut butter
75g (3oz/6 tbsp) butter at room temperature
180g (6½oz/scant 1 cup) soft brown sugar
2 large free-range eggs
150ml (5fl oz/⅔ cup) milk or almond milk
a few drops of vanilla extract
180g (6½oz/scant 2 cups) plain (all-purpose) flour
2 tsp baking powder
50g (2oz/scant ½ cup) chopped roasted peanuts
250g (9oz/1½ cups) dark (semi-sweet) chocolate chips
sea salt

Preheat the oven to 180°C (160°C fan)/350°F/gas 4. Line a 12-hole muffin tin (pan) with paper cases (liners).

Beat the peanut butter, butter and sugar together until soft and fluffy. It's easiest to use a food mixer for this. Beat in the eggs, one at a time, and then the milk and vanilla extract.

Sift in the flour, baking powder and a good pinch of salt. Fold gently into the mixture, using a figure-of-eight motion – or do this on the slowest speed if using a food mixer. Gently fold in the peanuts and chocolate chips, distributing them evenly throughout.

Spoon the mixture into the paper cases and cook in the preheated oven for 25–30 minutes until well risen and golden brown. Leave to cool on a wire cooling rack. The muffins will stay fresh in a tin or airtight container for 3–4 days.

BANANA MUFFINS WITH CRUNCHY CRUMBLE TOPPING

These muffins are made with nut butter and milk instead of dairy products, making them healthier and with fewer calories. Sprinkling some crumble mixture over the top makes them deliciously crunchy.

MAKES 12 MUFFINS
PREP 15 MINUTES
COOK 20 MINUTES

100g (4oz/scant ½ cup) almond butter
2 large ripe bananas
2 large free-range eggs
120ml (4fl oz/½ cup) almond milk
75g (3oz/scant ½ cup) soft brown sugar
2 tbsp ground almonds (almond meal)
250g (9oz/2½ cups) self-raising flour
1 tsp baking powder

CRUMBLE TOPPING
85g (3oz/generous ¼ cup) almond butter
50g (2oz/½ cup) rolled oats
50g (2oz/¼ cup) demerara sugar

Preheat the oven to 190°C (170°C fan)/375°F/gas 5. Line a 12-hole muffin tin (pan) with paper cases (liners).

Make the crumble topping: mix the ingredients together with a fork until they stick together and form crumbs.

Using a food mixer or hand-held electric whisk, beat the almond butter, bananas, eggs and milk until smooth. Gently stir in the sugar and ground almonds. Sift in the flour and baking powder and fold into the mixture in a figure-of-eight motion.

Spoon the mixture into the paper cases and sprinkle the crumble topping over them. Cook in the preheated oven for about 20 minutes until well risen and golden brown. Leave to cool on a wire cooling rack. The muffins will stay fresh in a tin or airtight container for 3–4 days.

HONEY AND ALMOND CAKE

This cake also makes a wonderful dessert. Just cut into squares or slices, top with a spoonful of crème fraîche, mascarpone or whipped cream and serve with fresh raspberries or strawberries.

SERVES 8
PREP 15 MINUTES
COOK 35–40 MINUTES

185g (6½oz/¾ cup) almond butter
125g (4oz/generous ½ cup) butter at room temperature
180ml (6½fl oz/¾ cup) clear honey, plus extra for drizzling
2 medium free-range eggs, beaten
125g (4½oz/1¼ cups) plain (all-purpose) flour
1 tsp baking powder
½ tsp bicarbonate of soda (baking soda)
½ tsp salt
75g (3oz/½ cup) ground almonds (almond meal)
3–4 tbsp flaked almonds

Preheat the oven to 180°C (160°C fan)/350°F/gas 4. Line a 20cm (8 inch) loose-bottomed tin (springform pan) with baking parchment.

Using a food mixer or hand-held electric whisk, beat the almond butter, butter and honey until smooth and well combined. Whisk in the beaten eggs.

Sift the flour, baking powder and bicarbonate of soda into the mixture. Add the salt and ground almonds and fold in gently with a metal spoon in a figure-of-eight motion until everything is incorporated evenly.

Spoon the mixture into the lined baking tin and sprinkle the flaked almonds over the top. Bake in the preheated oven for 35–40 minutes until the cake is risen and golden brown and springs back when you press it gently. To test whether it's cooked, insert a metal skewer into the centre – if it comes out clean, it's ready.

Leave to cool in the tin for 10 minutes before turning out onto a wire rack. Drizzle some honey over the warm cake and leave until it's completely cold and has absorbed the honey. Cut into slices to serve. Store in a tin or airtight container for up to 5 days.

QUICK NUT BUTTER APPLE TART

Adding some nut butter to a classic apple tart makes it more creamy. You could even use crunchy peanut butter or tuck some hazelnuts or flaked almonds in between the rows of apple.

SERVES 6–8
PREP 15 MINUTES
COOK 30–35 MINUTES

oil or butter, for greasing
flour, for dusting
250g (9oz) ready-rolled puff
　pastry, fresh or frozen and
　thawed
150g (5oz/⅔ cup) nut butter, e.g.
　almond or hazelnut
4 dessert apples, cored and thinly
　sliced
2 tbsp melted butter
4 tbsp caster (superfine) sugar
a pinch of ground cinnamon
75g (3oz/¼ cup) apricot jam
cream, crème fraîche or ice
　cream, to serve

Preheat the oven to 200°C (180°C fan)/400°F/gas 6. Lightly grease a baking tray (cookie sheet) with oil or butter.

Dust a clean work surface with flour and roll out the puff pastry thinly to a 20 x 30cm (8 x 12 inch) rectangle. Carefully transfer it to the greased baking tray and prick it all over with a fork.

Spread the nut butter over the pastry in an even layer, leaving a border of 2.5cm (1 inch) around the edge for the pastry to rise. Place the sliced apples in overlapping rows on top and brush with melted butter. Sprinkle lightly with the sugar and dust with cinnamon.

Bake in the preheated oven for 25–30 minutes until the apples are cooked and the pastry is crisp, golden brown and well risen.

Stir the apricot jam in a small pan set over a low heat until it's just warm and more liquid. Brush over the top of the apples and replace in the oven for 5 minutes.

Serve the tart, warm or at room temperature, cut into slices with cream, crème fraîche or ice cream.

NUT BUTTER CHOCOLATE CRÊPES

You can make the crêpes in advance and leave them to go cold before reheating in the microwave when you're ready to serve them. Try adding some strawberries, sliced peaches or juicy cherries.

SERVES 4–6
PREP 10 MINUTES
STAND 30 MINUTES
COOK 10 MINUTES

125g (4½oz/1¼ cups) plain (all-purpose) flour
2 tbsp caster (superfine) sugar
a pinch of salt
300ml (11fl oz/1¼ cups) milk
3 medium free-range eggs, beaten
a knob of butter or lard (shortening), for cooking
125g (4½oz/½ cup) nut butter, e.g. hazelnut or crunchy peanut butter
icing (confectioner's) sugar, for dusting

NUTTY CHOCOLATE SAUCE
125g (4½oz/½ cup) hazelnut chocolate spread, e.g. Nutella
4 tbsp single (light) cream

Make the crêpes: sift the flour into a bowl and stir in the sugar and salt. Make a hollow in the centre and whisk in a little of the milk. Beat in the remaining milk and eggs until you have a smooth batter. Alternatively, do this in a food processor.

Pour the batter into a jug and leave to stand for at least 30 minutes.

When you're ready to make the crêpes, grease a small non-stick frying pan or omelette pan with a little butter or lard and set over a medium to high heat. When it's really hot, pour in a little batter and swirl it around, tilting the pan to cover the base. Cook until the crêpe is set and golden brown underneath and the edges are starting to peel back, then flip it over and cook the other side. Remove from the pan and keep warm while you cook the remaining crêpes in the same way. You may need to add more butter or lard in between cooking them to prevent them sticking.

Make the nutty chocolate sauce: put the chocolate hazelnut spread in a small pan with the cream and stir gently over a low heat until well blended and melted. Alternatively, heat the chocolate hazelnut spread in the microwave and thin down with the cream.

Spread a little nut butter over each crêpe and fold it over or roll up. Serve warm dusted with icing sugar and drizzled with nutty chocolate sauce.

Tip: Stack the crêpes on a plate, as you cook them, with a sheet of greaseproof paper in between. Keep them warm in a low oven.

PEANUT APPLE CRUMBLE

If you've never thought of adding peanut butter to a crumble topping, think again. Most nut butters work well and you can throw in some chopped nuts, ground almonds and spices as well.

SERVES 4
PREP 15 MINUTES
COOK 30–35 MINUTES

butter, for greasing
1kg (2lb 4oz) cooking (green) apples, peeled, cored and sliced
50g (2oz/¼ cup) caster (superfine) sugar
3–4 tbsp cold water
1 tsp ground cinnamon
4 whole cloves
cream, crème fraîche, ice cream or custard, to serve

PEANUT BUTTER CRUMBLE

100g (4oz/1 cup) plain (all-purpose) flour
50g (2oz/½ cup) rolled porridge oats
50g (2oz/¼ cup) demerara sugar
75g (3oz/generous ¼ cup) crunchy peanut butter
50g (2oz/¼ cup) butter, diced

Preheat the oven to 190°C (170°C fan)/375°F/gas 5. Lightly butter a shallow ovenproof baking dish.

Make the peanut butter crumble: mix the flour, oats and sugar together in a large mixing bowl. Break the peanut butter into lumps and add to the bowl with the diced butter. Using your fingertips, rub in the two butters until the mixture resembles fine breadcrumbs.

Put the apples, sugar and 1 tablespoon of the water in a saucepan. Sprinkle with the cinnamon and stick the sharp ends of the cloves into some pieces of apple. Cook over a medium heat, stirring occasionally, for 5 minutes until the apples start to soften. When ready, tip them into the buttered baking dish. Add the remaining cold water and stir until the mixture starts to stick together.

Sprinkle the crumble mixture evenly over the apples, levelling the top, so they are completely covered. Bake in the preheated oven for 25–30 minutes until the topping is crisp and golden brown and the apples are cooked and tender.

Serve warm with cream, crème fraîche, ice cream or custard. This also tastes good eaten cold the following day.

VARIATIONS
• Instead of apples, use whatever fruit is in season – pears, cherries, blackberries, plums, greengages, apricots or even strawberries.

GLUTEN-FREE PEANUT BUTTER BANANA BREAD

You can enjoy this wonderfully moist banana bread with a cup of tea or coffee at any time of the day or eat it sliced and buttered for breakfast, Caribbean-style. Transform it into a teatime treat by drizzling it with lemony icing or topping with some peanut butter and soft cheese frosting.

SERVES 8
PREP 15 MINUTES
COOK 1 HOUR

3 ripe bananas
150g (5oz/⅔ cup) peanut butter
3 tbsp coconut oil, plus extra for greasing
180g (6½oz/scant 1 cup) soft brown sugar
2 large free-range eggs, beaten
4 tbsp almond milk
1 tsp vanilla extract
150g (5oz/1½ cups) gluten-free flour
1 tsp baking powder
½ tsp bicarbonate of soda (baking soda)
100g (4oz/scant ¾ cup) ground almonds (almond meal)
½ tsp salt
½ tsp ground cinnamon
½ tsp ground nutmeg
icing (confectioner's) sugar, for dusting

Preheat the oven to 180°C (160°C fan)/350°F/gas 4. Line an oiled 450g (1lb) loaf tin (pan) with baking parchment.

Beat the bananas, peanut butter, coconut oil and sugar together. Use a hand-held electric whisk or food mixer to make this easier. Beat in the eggs, almond milk and vanilla.

Sift in the flour, baking powder and bicarbonate of soda and gently fold into the mixture with the ground almonds, salt and ground spices. If the mixture is a little thick, just add some more almond milk to slacken it.

Pour the mixture into the lined loaf tin and bake in the preheated oven for about 1 hour until the loaf is well risen and golden brown. You can test whether it's ready by inserting a metal skewer into the centre – if it comes out clean, the banana bread is cooked.

Allow the loaf to cool in the tin for 10 minutes and then turn it out onto a wire rack. When it's completely cold, dust with icing sugar and cut into slices to serve. This loaf keeps well, wrapped in kitchen foil, for several days.

> Tip: This banana bread freezes well. Wrap it in foil and a plastic freezer bag and freeze for up to 3 months.

PEANUT BUTTER MILKSHAKE

Enjoy a peanut butter milkshake as a snack, a quick breakfast or as a dessert. You can vary the nut butters, even using chocolate hazelnut spread, such as Nutella or see the homemade version on page 16.

SERVES 2
PREP 5 MINUTES

1 banana, peeled and cut into chunks
250g (9oz/2 cups) vanilla ice cream
120ml (4fl oz/½ cup) cold milk
4 tbsp smooth peanut butter
ice cubes (optional)

Put all the ingredients in a blender and blitz until well blended and smooth.

Pour the milkshake into two tall glasses and drink immediately.

Note: You can make a vegan version with vegan vanilla ice cream and unsweetened almond milk.

FLAVOURINGS
· Try adding a pinch of ground cinnamon, a drizzle of honey, 1–2 drops of vanilla extract or some cocoa powder.

FROZEN ALMOND BUTTER BANANAS

Eat these crunchy frozen bananas at any time of the day – as a healthy snack, for breakfast or as a dessert. They are so easy to make and great to keep in your freezer during the hot summer months. You can use any nut butter or white or milk chocolate for dipping.

MAKES 4 BANANAS
PREP 10 MINUTES
COOK 2–3 MINUTES
FREEZE 2 HOURS

2 firm large bananas
50g (2oz/scant ¼ cup) almond butter
225g (8oz) dark (semi-sweet) chocolate, cut into pieces
1 tbsp vegetable oil
60g (2oz/½ cup) chopped nuts or coconut shreds

Line a baking tray (cookie sheet) with non-stick baking parchment or wax paper.

Cut each banana in half horizontally so you end up with four pieces. Take one piece and cut it in half lengthways. Sandwich the two halves together with the almond butter to make a banana 'sandwich'. Repeat with the remaining pieces of banana and almond butter. If wished you can gently push a wooden ice cream stick (popsicle stick) into one end.

Arrange on the lined baking tray and freeze for 1 hour until frozen solid.

Put the chocolate and oil in a heatproof bowl suspended over a pan of simmering water and stir gently until it melts. Alternatively, use the microwave.

Dip the frozen bananas in the chocolate and then into some nuts or coconut. Place on the lined baking tray and freeze for at least 1 hour until set. You can keep them frozen in an airtight container for up to 2 weeks.

PEANUT BUTTER CUPS

These wickedly delicious peanut butter cups are very rich and decadent. If you prefer just a sweet bite, use mini petit four foil cases and make 24 little cups to eat as a snack or serve with coffee after a meal.

MAKES 12 CUPS
PREP 20 MINUTES
COOK 6–8 MINUTES
FREEZE 45–60 MINUTES

700g (1lb 9oz/4 cups) dark (semi-sweet) chocolate chips
50g (2oz/¼ cup) icing (confectioner's) sugar
25g (1oz/2 tbsp) butter at room temperature
125g (4½oz/½ cup) smooth peanut butter

Line a 12-hole muffin tin (pan) with paper or foil cases (liners).

Melt half of the chocolate chips in a microwave or a heatproof bowl suspended over a pan of simmering water. Spoon the melted chocolate into the 12 paper or foil cases to cover the bases evenly. Put the muffin tin in the freezer for 15–20 minutes until the chocolate sets hard.

While the chocolate is freezing, beat the sugar, butter and peanut butter in a food mixer or with a hand-held electric whisk in a bowl until creamy and smooth.

Remove the tin from the freezer and divide the peanut butter mixture between the paper cups, gently smoothing them over the chocolate layer to cover them evenly. Return to the freezer for 15–20 minutes.

Melt the remaining chocolate chips (as above) and spoon over the top of the peanut butter in a single layer to cover the top evenly. Return to the freezer for 15–20 minutes until set.

Store the peanut butter cups in a container in the fridge for up to 1 week. Serve them chilled or at room temperature.

INDEX

INDEX